S0-BKM-230

MUSICANADA 3

Penny Louise Brooks

Betty Anne Kovacs

Mary Martin Trotter

Contributing Author
Doreen Dunne Sunderland

General Editor
Penny Louise Brooks

HOLT, RINEHART AND WINSTON OF CANADA, LIMITED TORONTO.

MUSICANADA 3

Penny Louise Brooks
Independent Consultant, Music and Language Arts
Toronto, Ontario

Betty Anne Kovacs
Music Consultant
Etobicoke Board of Education
Etobicoke, Ontario

Mary Martin Trotter
Music Teacher
Elgin County Board of Education
St. Thomas, Ontario

Doreen Dunne Sunderland
Music Consultant
Renfrew County Board of Education
Pembroke, Ontario

ISBN 03-923178-X

Sponsoring Editor Sheba Meland
Developmental Editor Penny L. Brooks
Art Director Wycliffe Smith
Designer Jim Ireland
Illustrator Barbara Klunder
Cover Illustration Terry Shoffner

Canadian Cataloguing in Publication Data
Main entry under title:
Musicanada 3

For use in grade 3.
Includes index.
ISBN 0-03-923178-X

1. School music – Instruction and study – Canada.
2. Music – Instruction and study – Canada – Juvenile.
I. Brooks, Penny, 1950-

MT930.M873 372.8'7049 C82-094234-0

The authors and publisher thank the following educators for contributing valuable commentary during the development of this program:

Margaret Barnes
Music Specialist
Calgary Board of Education
Calgary, Alberta

Barbara Clark
Vocal Music Consultant
Ottawa Board of Education
Ottawa, Ontario

Lorraine Dalgliesh
Music Specialist
Calgary Board of Education
Calgary, Alberta

Peggy Emmond
Music Specialist
St. Boniface School Division #4
Winnipeg, Manitoba

Terry English
Music Consultant
Waterloo County Separate School Board
Kitchener, Ontario

Norine Inkster
Elementary Music Specialist
Calgary Board of Education
Calgary, Alberta

Isabelle Mills
Assistant Dean, College of Arts and Science
University of Saskatchewan
Saskatoon, Saskatchewan

Yvonne Navratil
Music Resource Teacher
Ottawa Board of Education
Ottawa, Ontario

Susan Scott
Music Resource Teacher
Ottawa Board of Education
Ottawa, Ontario

Brenda Trafford
Music Specialist
District 14 School Board
Sackville, New Brunswick

Dennis Tupman
Performing Arts Co-ordinator
Vancouver Board of Education
Vancouver, British Columbia

Rhonda Wicks
Music Co-ordinator
The Avalon Consolidated School Board
St. Johns, Newfoundland

Printed in Canada 2 3 4 5 86 85 84 83 82

CONTENTS

AUTUMN

WINTER

SPRING

AUTUMN

ZIP-A-DEE-DOO-DAH

Rote Song

Allie Wrubel

C: d' s m d m s d'
1 2 3 sing

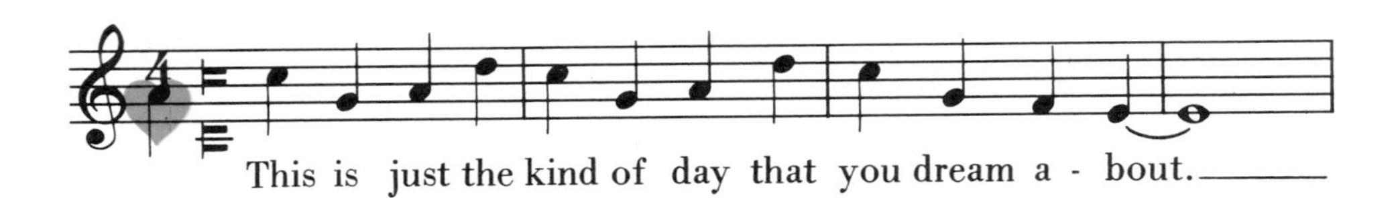
This is just the kind of day that you dream a - bout.

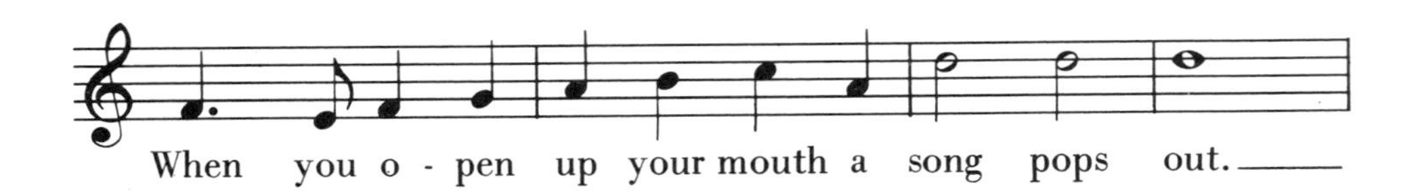
When you o - pen up your mouth a song pops out.

Chorus
Zip - a-dee - doo - dah, Zip - a-dee- ay!

My, oh my, what a won-der - ful day.

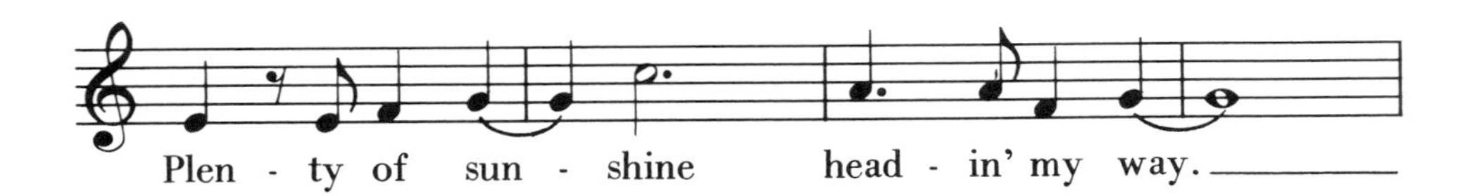
Plen - ty of sun - shine head - in' my way.

Zip - a dee - doo - dah, Zip - a-dee - ay! Mis - ter

Blue - bird on my shoul - der, It's the
truth, it's "act-ch'll," Ev'-ry-thing is "sa - tis-fact-ch'll."
Zip - a-dee - doo - dah, Zip - a-dee - ay!
Won - der-ful feel - ing, Won-der- ful day.

POLLY WOLLY DOODLE

Rote Song

American Folk Song

G: d m s m d
1 2 3 4 1 2 sing

G
1. Oh, I went down South for to see my Sal, Sing-ing
2. Oh, my Sal, she is a ___ maid - en fair, Sing-ing

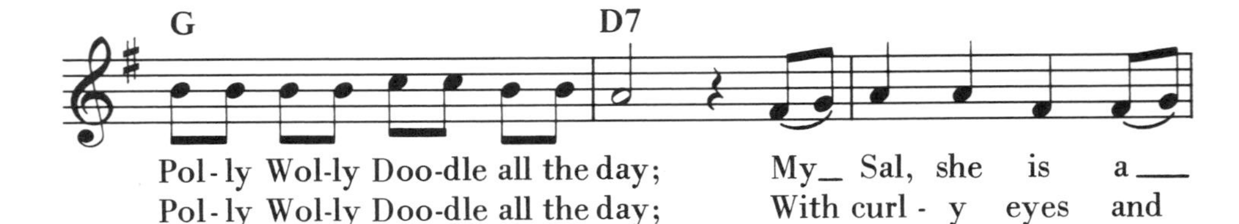
G
D7
Pol - ly Wol-ly Doo-dle all the day; My ___ Sal, she is a ___
Pol - ly Wol-ly Doo-dle all the day; With curl - y eyes and

D7
G
Chorus
spunk - y gal, Sing-ing Pol-ly Wol-ly Doo-dle all the day,
laugh - ing hair, Sing-ing Pol-ly Wol-ly Doo-dle all the day,
Fare thee

G
well, fare thee well, Fare thee well, my fair - y

D7
fay, For I'm goin' to Loui - si - an - a, for to

D7
G
see my Su-sy-an-na, Sing-ing Pol-ly Wol-ly Doo-dle all the day.

3. Oh, a grasshopper sittin' on a railroad track. . .
A-pickin' his teeth with a carpet tack. . .

4. Oh, I went to bed, but it wasn't no use. . .
My feet stuck out for the chickens to roost. . .

5. Behind the barn, down on my knees. . .
I thought I heard a chicken sneeze. . .

6. He sneezed so hard with the whooping cough. . .
He sneezed his head and tail right off. . .

EGG BEATER

M. Trotter

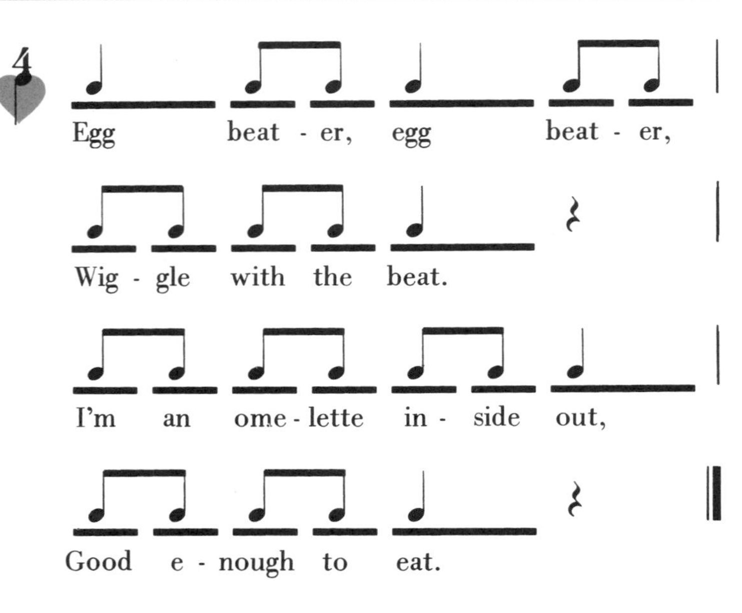

Egg beat - er, egg beat - er,
Wig - gle with the beat.
I'm an ome - lette in - side out,
Good e - nough to eat.

Where are the long sounds?
Where are the short sounds?

Make up actions that go with the beat.

Where are the strong beats?
Where are the silent beats?

Find the bar lines that group the beats.

says: There are 4 beats in every bar.
Every ♩ note gets one beat.

♫ = 1 beat

♩ = 1 beat

𝅗𝅥 = 2 beats

𝅝 = 4 beats

A rest 𝄽 is a silent beat.

The STOP sign in music is the double bar line.

Find the double bar line.

STOP

ALOUETTE

Rote Song

Canadian Folk Song

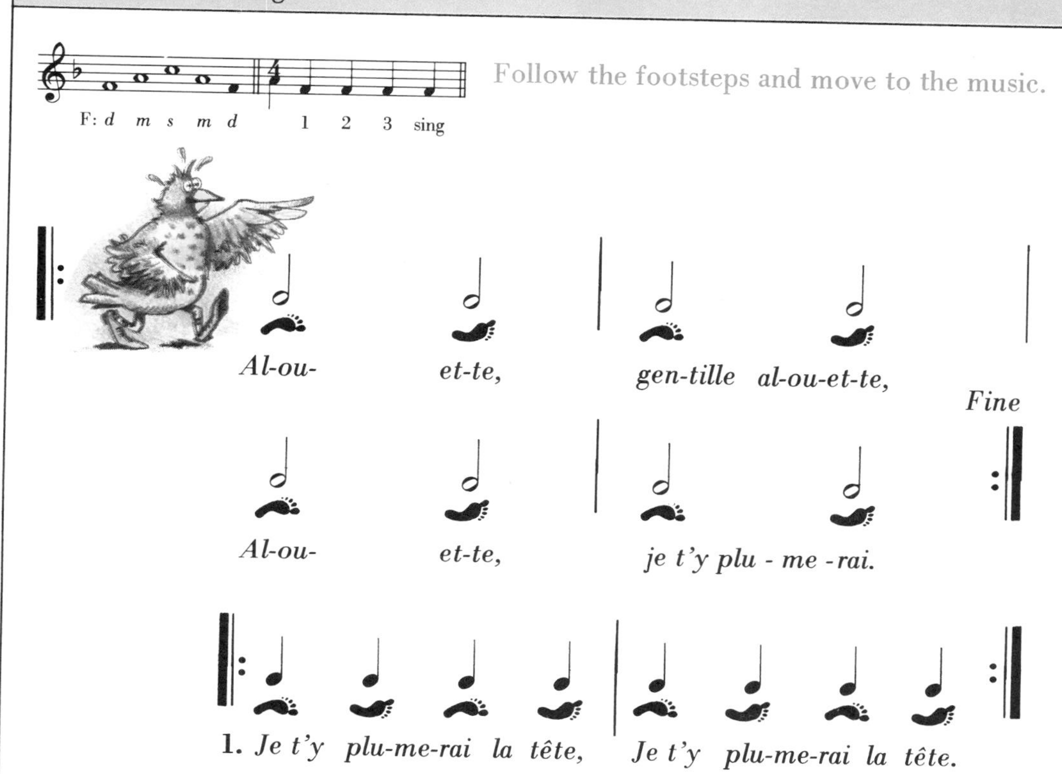
F: d m s m d
1 2 3 sing
Follow the footsteps and move to the music.
Al-ou- et-te, gen-tille al-ou-et-te,
Fine
Al-ou- et-te, je t'y plu - me -rai.
1. Je t'y plu-me-rai la tête, Je t'y plu-me-rai la tête.

D.C.
Et la tête,___ Al - ou - ette, Oh______

2. *Je t'y plu-me-rai le bec. . .*
3. *Je t'y plu-me-rai le nez. . .*
4. *Je t'y plu-me-rai les yeux. . .*
5. *Je t'y plu-me-rai le cou. . .*
6. *Je t'y plu-me-rai les ailes. . .*
7. *Je t'y plu-me-rai le dos. . .*
8. *Je t'y plu-me-rai les pattes. . .*
9. *Je t'y plu-me-rai la queue. . .*

𝄆 REPEAT 𝄇 This sign tells you to repeat a section of the song.

Have a leader sing the first time.
Sing the repeat together.

THE BIRTHDAY CHILD

Rote Song

Music by B. Andress/Lyrics traditional

D: d' s m d
1 2 3 sing

Clap the rhythm of the words and step the beat.

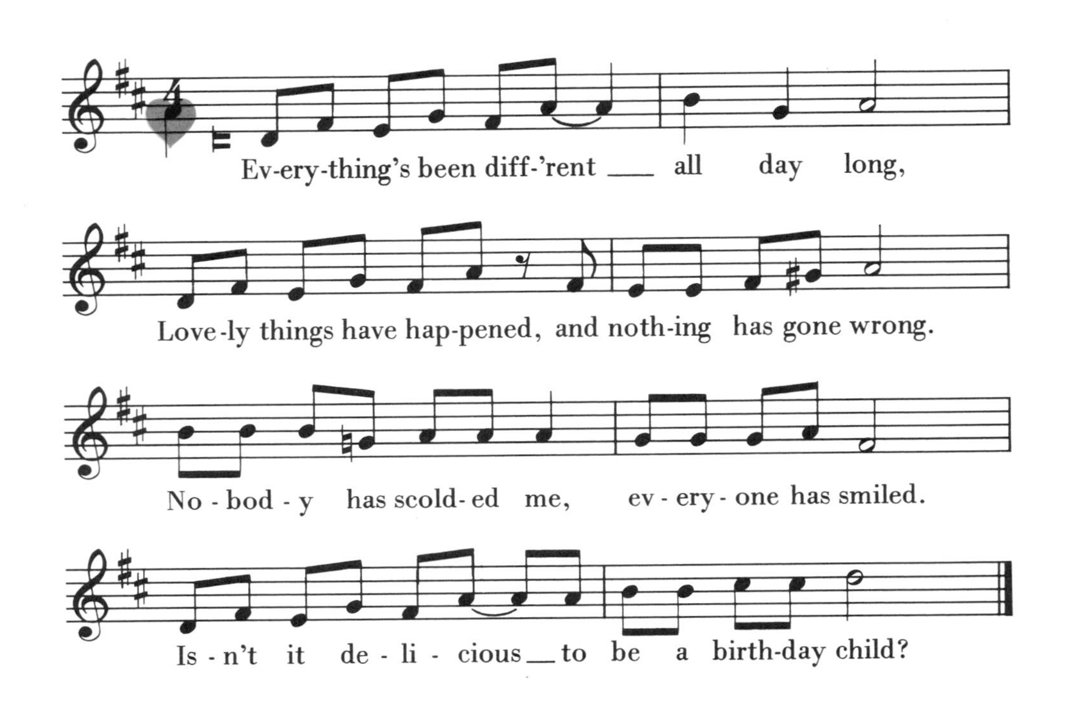
Ev-ery-thing's been diff-'rent ___ all day long,
Love-ly things have hap-pened, and noth-ing has gone wrong.
No - bod - y has scold- ed me, ev - ery - one has smiled.
Is - n't it de - li - cious __ to be a birth-day child?

Read the rhythm. Find the silent beats 𝄽 .

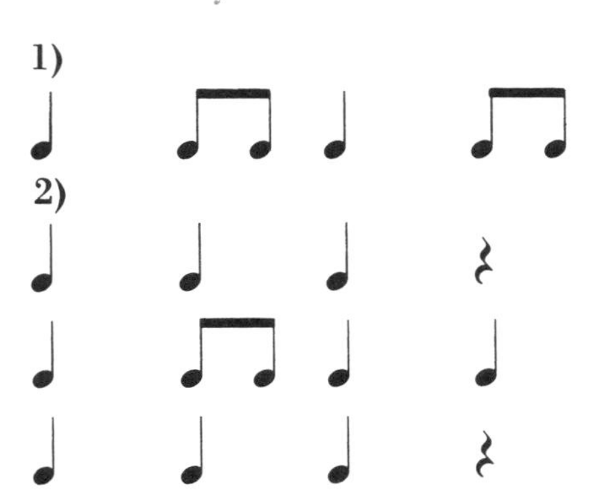
1)
2)

What do we do with the birthday child?

Give him a pinch to grow an inch!

Divide into two groups.
  Say the words as a round.
  When group I begins line 2, group II joins in.
  Think the words as one group taps and the other claps the rhythm.

THE STAFF

The staff is like an apartment building where the notes live. Notes can live on lines or in spaces.

How many lines are there on the staff? (Count from the bottom up).
How many spaces are there on the staff? (Count from the bottom up).

⊧ is a **doh** finder.

It is the "key" to the staff and tells where **doh** lives.

Where does **doh** live on this staff?

Where does **doh** live on this staff?

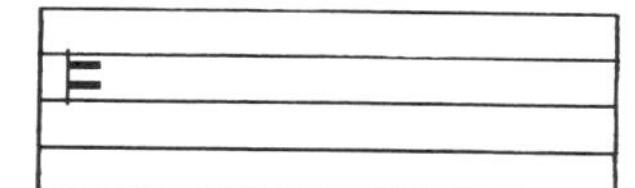

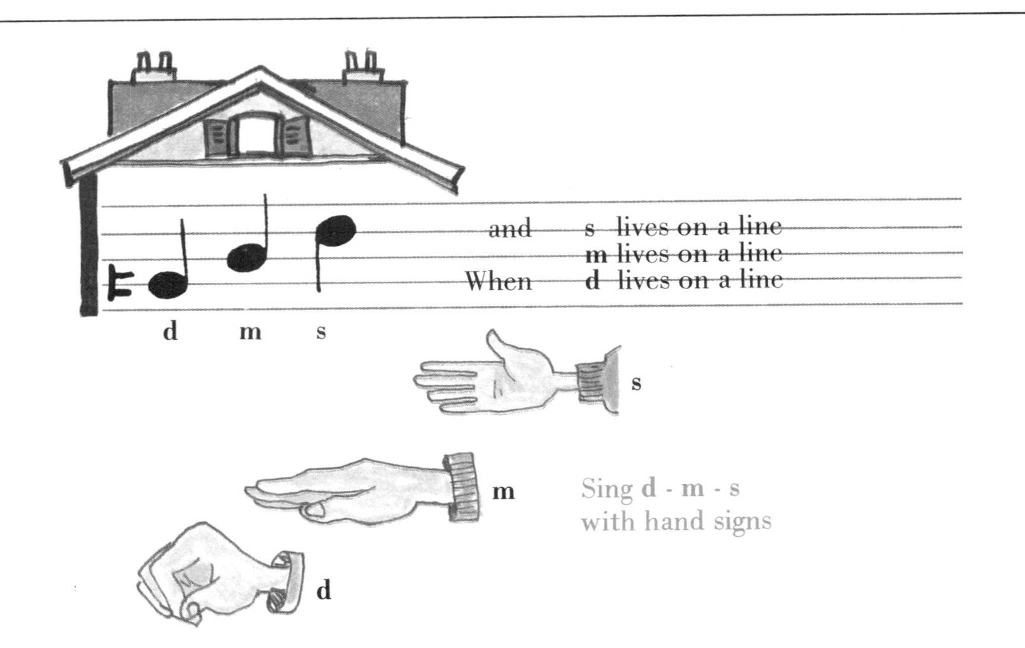
and s lives on a line
m lives on a line
When d lives on a line
d m s
s
m
d

Sing **d** - **m** - **s**
with hand signs

JOHNNY ONE HAMMER

Note Song

Game Song

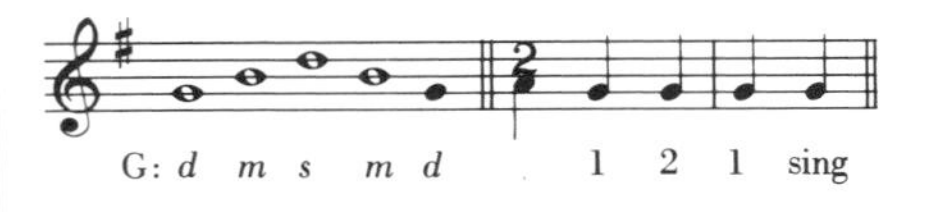
G: d m s m d
1 2 1 sing

Use the doh finder or key sign.
Is **doh** on a line or in a space?
Which one?
Where are **mi** and **soh**?

John-ny plays with one ham-mer, one ham-mer, one ham-mer,

John-ny plays with one ham-mer, then he plays with two.

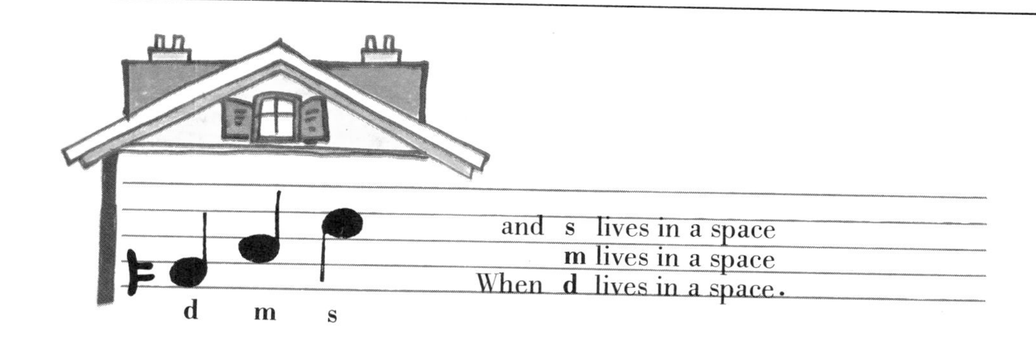
and s lives in a space
m lives in a space
When d lives in a space.
d m s

SAUTE LE PANTIN

Note/Rote Song

French/English Lyrics by M. Trotter

F: d m s m d 1 2 1 sing

Sau - te le pan-tin, sau - te le pan-tin. Il
Jump up, dance and play. Jump up, dance and play. Oh,
sau - te de son lit, il sau - te de son lit.
jump out of your bed, oh jump out of your bed.
Oh, tu es mon pan-tin, mon tout pe - tit pan-tin.
Oh, la - zy pup-pet, you're a sleep-y, sleep-y head.

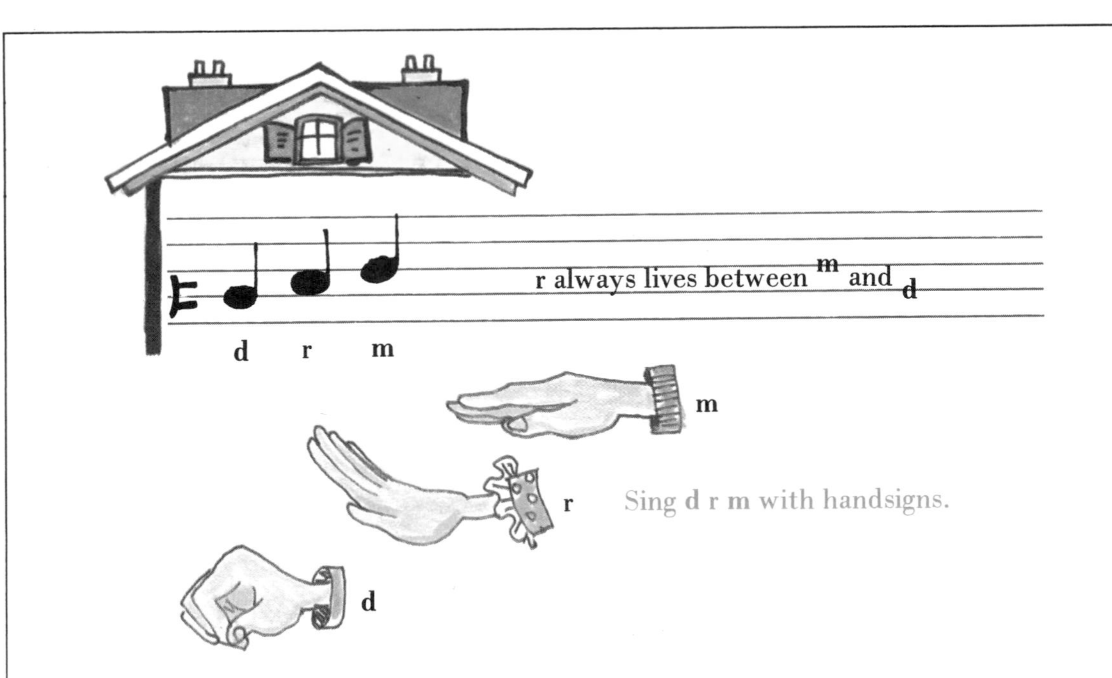
d r m
r always lives between m and d
m
r
d

Sing **d r m** with handsigns.

LONG-LEGGED LIFE

Note Song

Camp Song

G: d m s m r d
1 2 sing

Did you ev - er, ev - er, ev - er in your long - leg - ged life
No, I nev - er, nev - er, nev - er in my long - leg - ged life

Meet a long - leg - ged sail - or with a long - leg - ged wife?
Met a long - leg - ged sail - or with a long - leg - ged wife.

2
bow-legged life
3
four-legged life
4
short-legged life

COY MALINDO

Note/Rote Song

American Folk Song

F: d m s m d
1 2 3 4 1 2 sing

Use ⊨ to find **doh**.

On what note does the chorus begin?

Sing the chorus using handsigns.

1. I spurred my horse to make him trot,
2. I grabbed those reins and pulled them tight,
I spurred my horse to make him trot,
I grabbed those reins and pulled them tight,
I spurred my horse to make him trot,
I grabbed those reins and pulled them tight,
He jumped and ran like he was shot!
And rode that horse with all my might!
Chorus
Coy Ma-lin - do, Kill - ko - kill - ko, Coy Ma-lin - do, Kill - ko me.
Coy Ma-lin - do, Kill - ko - kill - ko, Coy Ma-lin - do, Kill - ko - me.

3. I fed my horse in a water trough, (3)
And there he got the whooping cough.

4. I fed my horse with a silver spoon, (3)
And then he kicked it over the moon.

5. When my horse is dead and gone, (3)
I'll use his jawbone to plow my corn.

LUKEY'S BOAT

Note/Rote Song

Canadian Folk Song

G: d m s m' d s,
1 2 3 4 1 2 sing

How many 3 beat notes 𝅗𝅥. can you find in this song?

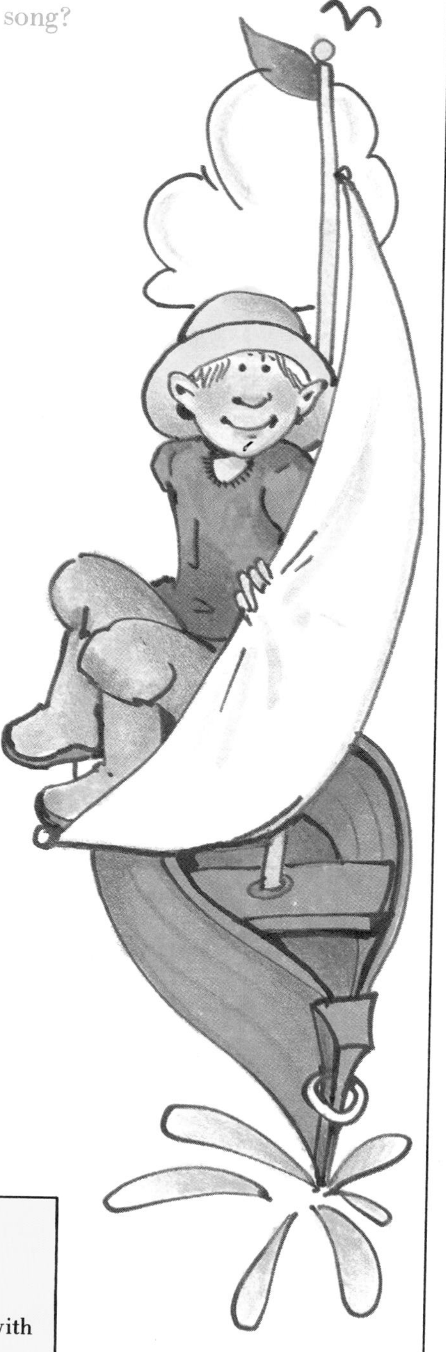

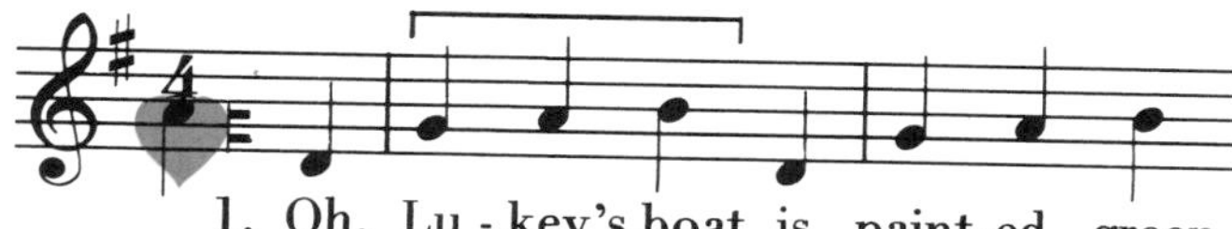
1. Oh, Lu - key's boat is paint-ed green,
2. Oh, Lu - key's sail - ing down the shore,

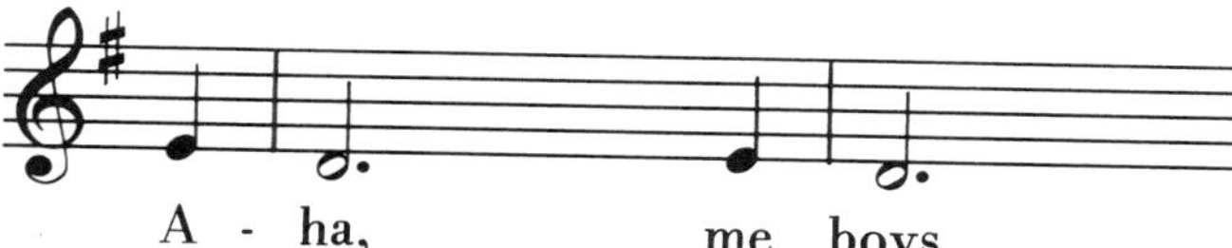
A - ha, me boys,
A - ha, me boys,

Oh, Lu - key's boat is paint - ed green,
Oh, Lu - key's sail - ing down the shore,

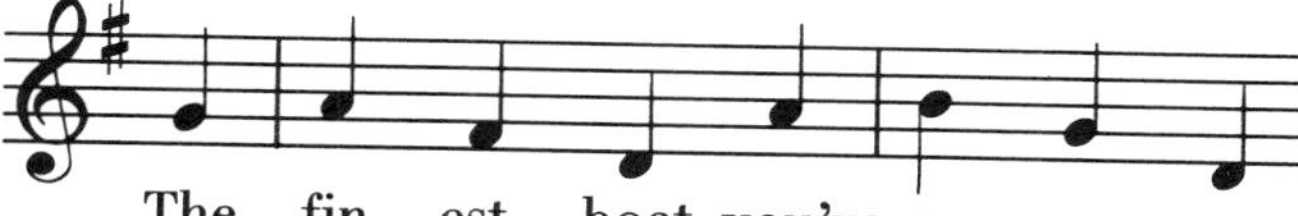
The fin - est boat you've ev - er seen,
To catch some fish from Lab - ra - dor,

A - ha, me rid-dle di - day!
A - ha, me rid-dle di - day!

3. Oh, Lukey's boat has cotton sails. . .
And planks put down with galvanized nails. . .

4. Oh, Lukey's rolling out his grub. . .
A barrel, a bag, a ten-pound tub. . .

BE A DETECTIVE:

How many times is **d r m** hidden in the song?
Now, make up a new verse one.
Wherever you found **d r m** sing the syllables with handsigns instead of words.

m
r
d
r always lives between m and d
m
r
d

Sing m r d with handsigns.

HOT CROSS BUNS

Note Song

Traditional

F: d r m s m
1 2 1 sing

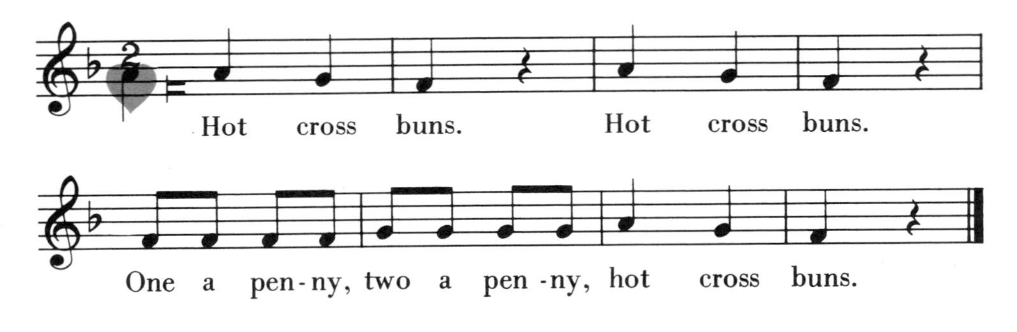
Hot cross buns. Hot cross buns.
One a pen-ny, two a pen -ny, hot cross buns.

AUTUMN

Rote Song

Bulgarian Melody/English Lyrics by Charles Winter

D: d' s m d m s
1 2 1 sing

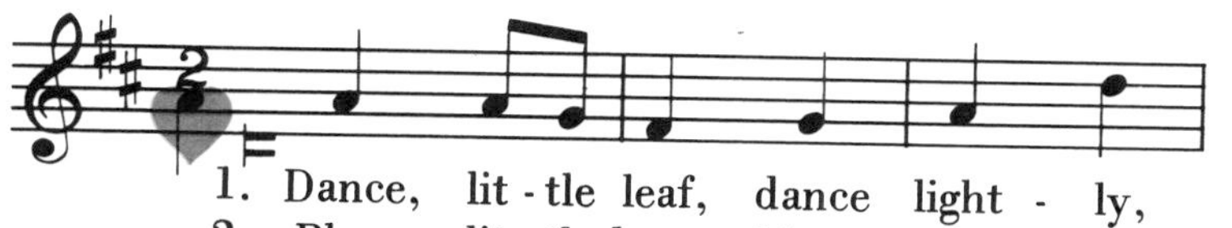

1. Dance, lit - tle leaf, dance light - ly,
2. Blow, lit - tle breeze, blow strong - er,
3. Then will the snow - flakes light go,

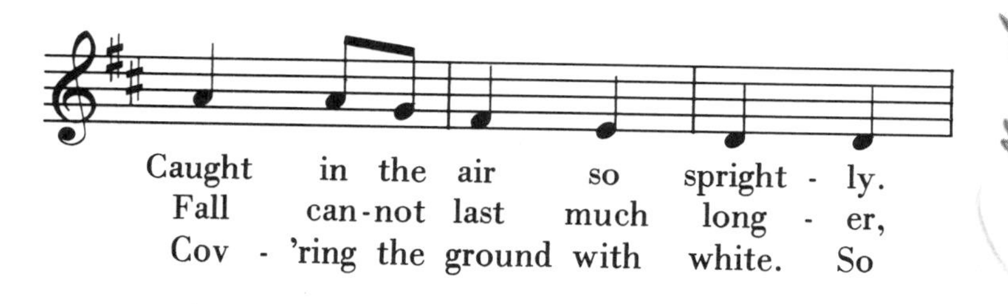

Caught in the air so spright - ly.
Fall can-not last much long - er,
Cov - 'ring the ground with white. So

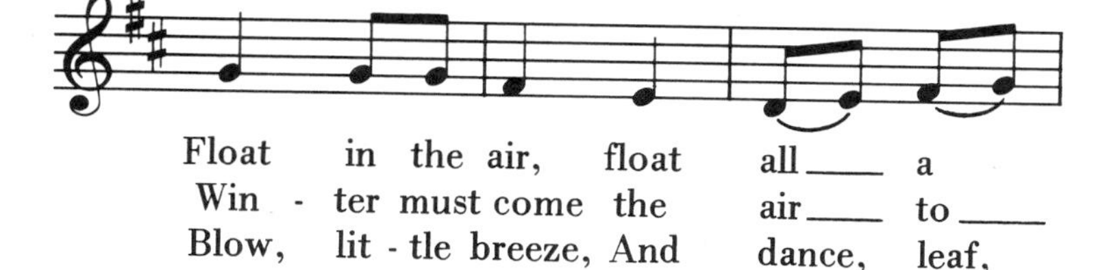

Float in the air, float all ___ a
Win - ter must come the air ___ to ___
Blow, lit - tle breeze, And dance, leaf,

round, Till you reach the ground. ___
fill, With an i - cy chill. ___
dance, While you have the chance. Dance!

ALISON'S CAMEL

Rote Song

Game Song

F: d m s m r d
1 2 3 sing

F
1. Al - i - son's cam - el has ten humps,
2. Al i - son's cam - el has nine humps,
C7
F
Al - i - son's cam - el has ten humps, Al - i - son's cam - el has
Al - i - son's cam - el has nine humps, Al - i son's cam - el has
B♭7
C7
F
C7
ten humps, so go, Al - i - son, go. Boom, boom, boom.
nine humps, so go, Al - i - son, go. Boom, boom, boom.

3. eight humps . . .
4. seven humps . . .
5. six humps . . .
6. five humps . . .
7. four humps . . .
8. three humps . . .
9. two humps . . .
10. one hump . . .

11. Alison's camel has no humps, (3)
So Alison's camel is a horse—of course.

TET TROOM TOO

Rote Song

Vietnamese Folk Song/English Lyrics by M. Trotter

Vietnamese children celebrate autumn by watching the full moon rise at midnight. After a candlelight parade, they sit in a circle surrounded by a fence of lanterns to play games, sing, and eat in the moonlight.

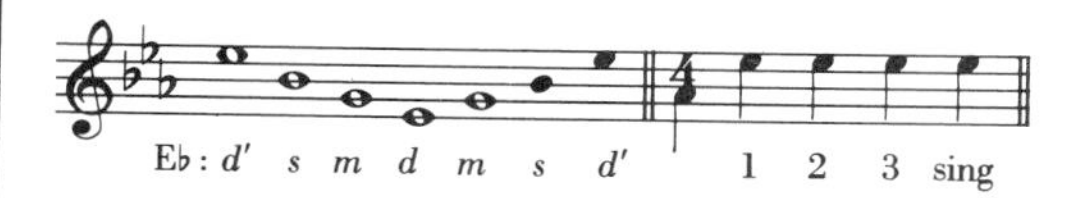

E♭: d' s m d m s d'
1 2 3 sing

Tet troom too dope dang dee choy, Em dope dang dee cup foh foong

Lowm voy soong voy_dang troom tye, Em mooah ka youee ahn drung drum.

Dang oum sahw voy dang ka chep, Dang tin nya voi dang boom boom
Tome yin yin kak tome yin yin, Tome yin yin kak tome yin yin

1.
2.
Em sat dang nahee done koom trang.
Em sat dang nahee
done chee Hang.

Full moon as you rise tonight,
I will light my candle bright.
From my lantern it will glow,
Marching through the streets below.

"Tome yin yin kak," sound the drum!
"Tome yin yin kak," children come!
Show the moon maid up above.

THE PENTATONIC SCALE

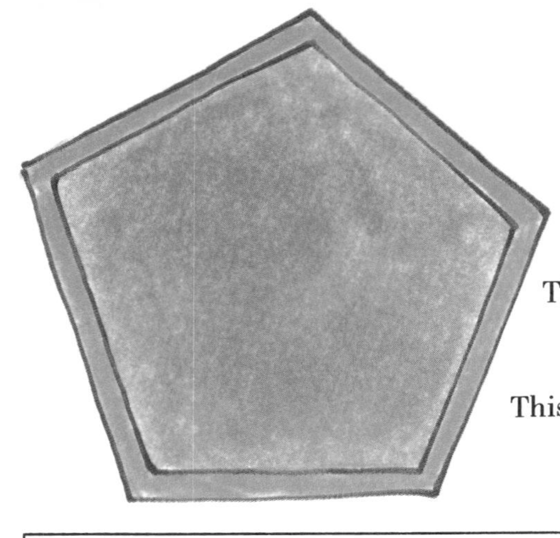

This is a penta gon.
How many sides does it have?

This is a penta tonic scale.
How many notes does it have?
What does penta mean?

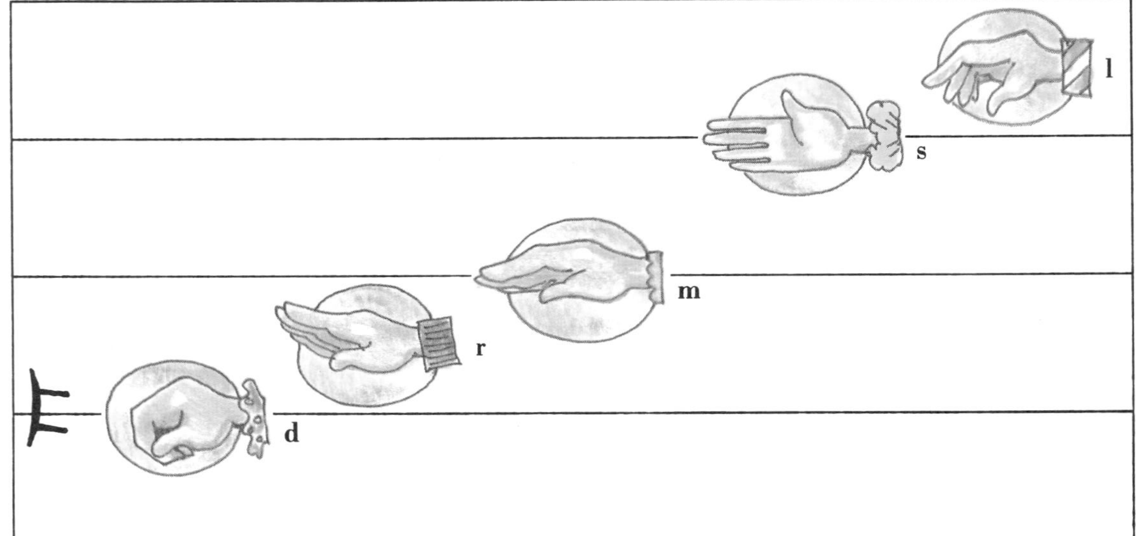

l
s
m
r
d

Find the pentatonic scale on the piano.
What keys will you use?
What group is **d r m**? What group is **s l**?

BE A DETECTIVE:
Find the notes that move by step.
Find the skip.

ROCKY MOUNTAIN

Note Song

American Folk Song

G: d m s m d
1 2 1 sing

What notes are used in this song?
What kind of scale do they make?

1. Rock - y moun-tain, rock-y moun-tain, rock-y moun-tain high,
2. Sun - ny val - ley, sun - ny val - ley, sun - ny val - ley low,
3. Storm-y o-cean, storm-y o-cean, storm-y o-cean wide,

When you're on that rock-y moun-tain, hang your head and cry.
When you're in that sun-ny val - ley, sing it soft and low.
When you're on that deep blue sea, there's no place you can hide.

Chorus

Do, do, do, do, do re - mem-ber me,

Do, do, do, do, do re - mem-ber me.

Play this song on the piano.
What keys will you use?

FOR HEALTH AND STRENGTH

Rote Song and Round

Traditional

G: d m s m d s,
1 2 3 4 1 2 sing

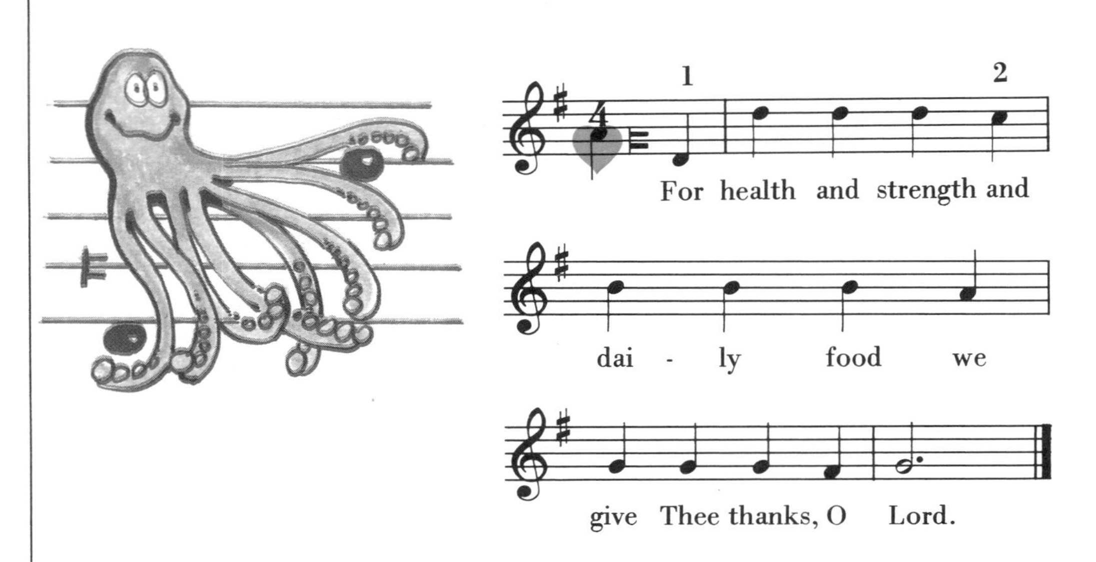
1
2
For health and strength and
dai - ly food we
give Thee thanks, O Lord.

COLOUR A RAINBOW

Dorothy Cameron Smith

Colour a rainbow
sparkle a star
colour a rainbow
wherever you are.
Life is a colouring book
given to you,
use the bright crayons
all the way through.

Use the light accents
of laughter and song,
you'll have a picture
that's right and not wrong.
Colour a rainbow
sparkle a star
colour a rainbow
wherever you are.

IROQUOIS LULLABY

Note Song

Native Peoples' Song/English Lyrics by M. Trotter

Em(G): d t, l, d m d l, d m
1 2 3 sing

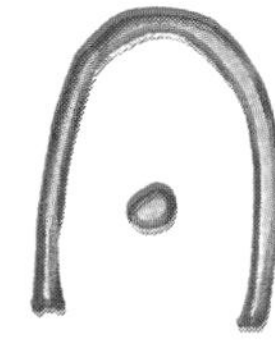

A fermata tells you to hold the sound longer than usual.

1. Ho, Ho,— Wa-ta-nay, Ho, Ho,— Wa-ta-nay,
2. Slum - ber, my lit-tle one, Slum - ber, my lit-tle one,
3. Do, do,— mon pe-tit, Do, do,— mon pe-tit,

Ho, Ho,— Wa-ta-nay, Ki-yo-ke-na, Ki-yo-ke-na.
Slum - ber, my lit-tle one and gen-tly sleep, so gen-tly sleep.
Do, do,— mon pe-tit et bon-ne nuit, et bon-ne nuit.

together
separated

BEDTIME STORIES

Poem

Lilian Moore

"Tell me a story,"
Says Witch's Child.

"About the Beast
So fierce and wild.

About a Ghost
That shrieks and groans.

A Skeleton
That rattles bones.

About a Monster
Crawly-creepy.

Something nice
To make me sleepy."

Use your voice in special ways to make this poem sound exciting.

How many ways can you use your voice?

high - low?
loud - soft?
fast - slow?

SKIN AND BONES

Note/Rote Song

American Folk Song

Em(G): d t, l, d m d l,
1 2 1 sing

Legato (smoothly)

1. There was an old wom-an all skin and bones, Oo - oo - oo-ooh!
2. She lived down by___ the old grave-yard, Oo - oo - oo-ooh!

3. One night she thought she'd take a walk,
4. She walked down by the old graveyard,
5. She saw the bones a-layin' around,
6. She went to the closet to get a broom,
7. She opened the door and BOO!!!

Some songs use **lah** and **soh** below **doh.**

How many low **lah's (lah,)** are there?
How many low **soh's (soh,)** are there?

FIVE LITTLE PUMPKINS

Note/Rote Song

Music by Charles Winter

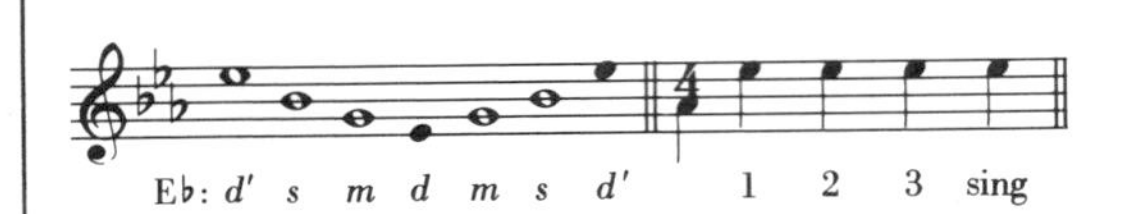

E♭: d' s m d m s d'
1 2 3 sing

d' t l s
Five lit - tle pump - kins sit - ting on a gate,
f m r d
The first one said, "Oh, my, it's get - ting late."
The sec - ond one said, "There are witch-es in the air."
r r r
The third one said, "But we don't care."
m m

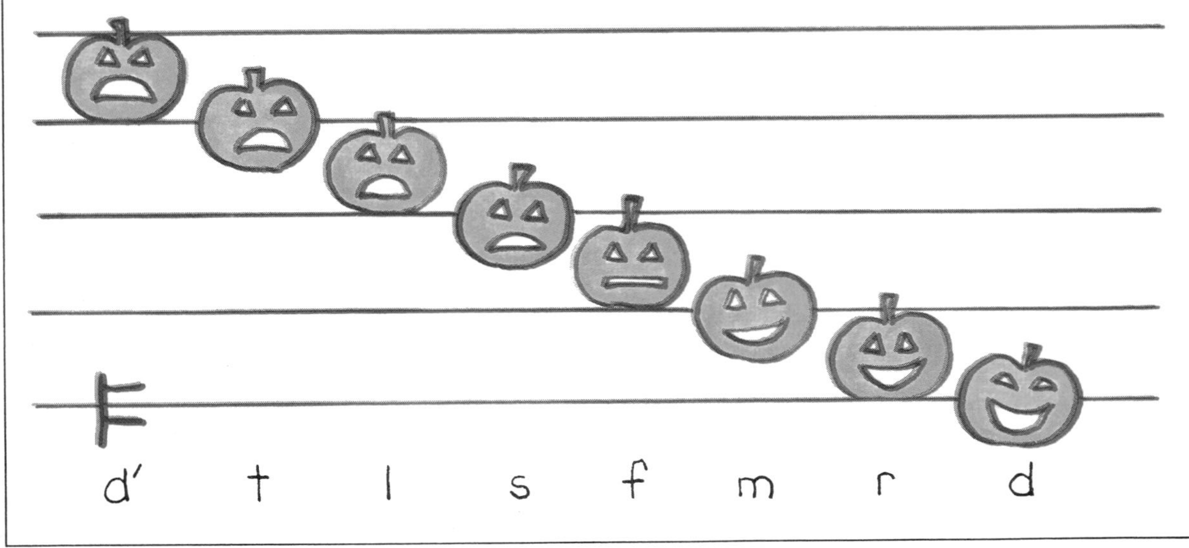

d' t l s f m r d

d′
t
l
s
f
m
r
d
The fourth one said, "Let's run and run and run."
f f
The fifth one said, "I'm read - y for some fun."
s s
"Oo - oo!" went the wind and out went the light,
And the five lit - tle pump - kins rolled out of sight.

HALLOWE'EN NIGHT

Rote Song

Hungarian Melody/ Lyrics by V. Russell and M. Trotter

Em(G): d t, l, l, d m
1 2 3 sing
Em
Am
Em
1. Big, black cats, Pump-kin fac - es too,
2. Gob - lins, ghosts, sli-ding through the sky,
Em
Am
Em
Star - ing eyes, Owls are watch-ing you.
Ride the wind, sil - ent - ly they fly.
Em
Em
Witch-es ri - ding broom-sticks, Past a moon so bright.
Sha-dows climb-ing walls 'neath Jack - o - lan-tern light.
Em
B
Em
'Tis a spook-y sight on Hal-low-e'en night!
3. Ring the bell; Knock at ev'ry door.
"Shelling out," Always room for more.
Where are all the ghosts from?
Watch them take their flight.
BE A DETECTIVE:
Find bars that are the same.

WINNIE THE WITCH

Rote Song

Barbara Andress

Dm(F): d t, l, d m d l, 1 2 3 1 2 sing

1. Win - nie the witch all with-ered and wrin-kled,
(2.) tapped at the door and rat - tled the roofs,__ She

Rode on a broom o'er the town of Tam - win - kle.
cack - led and danced in___ black smo - ky poofs.__

She flew_by the win- dows and brushed with her broom,
She prac-ticed be - ing wick - ed but try___ as she might,

1.

She peeked at the chil- dren a sleep in their rooms. **2.** She
The chil- dren all loved her on

2.

Hal - lo - we'en night!

Use these changes to make the song spooky:

Soft
p
LOUD!
f
Soft
p

IN A DARK WOOD

Tap a steady beat.

4

ff	In a dark, dark wood, there was a dark, dark house,	*p*	And in that dark, dark cupboard, there was a dark, dark shelf,
f	And in that dark, dark house, there was a dark, dark room,	*pp*	And on that dark, dark shelf, there was a dark, dark box,
mf	And in that dark, dark room, there was a dark, dark cupboard,	*ppp*	And in that dark, dark box, there was a

fff GHOST!

LITTLE TOMMY TINKER

Note Song and Round

Traditional

C: d' m s d
1 2 3 sing

1
Lit- tle Tom-my Tin - ker sat up - on a clink - er,

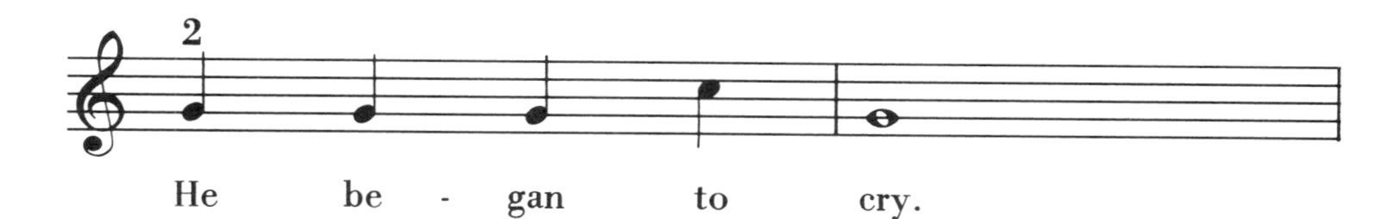
2
He be - gan to cry.

3
Ma, ______ Ma, ______

4
Poor lit - tle in - no - cent guy.

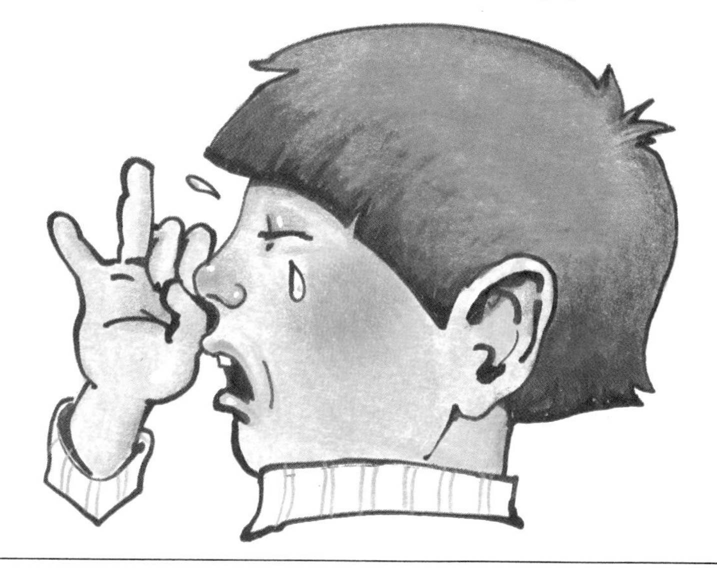

JIM ALONG JOSIE

Note Song

American Folk Song

F: d m s m d m s
1 2 3 sing

Chorus
F C F
Hey, come a - long, jim a - long Jo - sie.
F C F F
Hey, come a-long, jim a - long Joe. Hey, come a-long,
C F F C F
Fine
jim a-long Jo - sie. Hey, come a - long, jim a-long Joe.
1. Face to the cen - tre, hands on your knees.
2. There's a young la - dy, sweet as can be.
3. Asked her to mar-ry me, one fine sum-mer day.
D.C. al Fine
Clap three times and turn a - round please.
When we change part - ners, she'll be with me.
She was too bu sy, and went on her way.

This song uses high **doh′**.
How many can you find?
Where are they?

d **d′**

THE CONDUCTOR

This is a conductor.

A conductor shows strong and weak beats in music with arm movements.

For songs with two beats in each bar, the beats look like this:

1
strong
2
weak

LISTENING:

"Entertainer Rag"

Scott Joplin

This piece of music is performed by the "Canadian Brass," one of Canada's best-known ensembles. An **ensemble** is a group of musicians that makes music together. This one includes

- two trumpets,
- one french horn
- one trombone and
- one tuba.

Conduct as you listen to the piece.
How does the **tempo** or speed change?
Use your ear to help you find the strong beats.

DONKEY RIDING

Rote Song

Canadian Folk Song

This song was sung by sailors loading Quebec timber to be taken to Great Britain. The "donkey" in this song is not an animal, but the engine used to help load the cargo onto the ship.

E♭ : d' m s d
1 2 1 sing

Happily
1. Were you ev - er in Que- bec Stow-ing tim - ber on a deck, Where there's a king with a gol - den crown,
2. Were you ev - er off the Horn Where it's al - ways fine and warm, See - ing the lion and the U - ni - corn,
3. Were you ever in Car - diff Bay Where the folks all shout Hur - ray! Here comes John with his three months' pay,"
Rid - ing on a don - key? Hey, ho! A- way we go! Don - key rid - ing, don - key rid - ing.
Hey,— ho! A-way we go! Rid-ing on a don - key.

The **accent** > shows you where to emphasize notes to make the rhythm exciting.
Conduct while you sing the song.

DOBBIN, DOBBIN

Rote Song

Max and Beatrice Krone

F: d m s m d
1 2 3 sing

1. Dob - bin, Dob - bin, on your way.
2. Dob - bin, Dob - bin, don't you stop.
We've been to-geth-er for man-y a day, So let your
Just let your feet go clip-pe-ty clop, And let your
tail go swish as the wheels go 'round,
tail go swish as the wheels go 'round,
Chorus
Gid-dy - ap! We're home - ward bound.
Gid-dy - ap! We're home - ward bound.
I like to

*
take a horse and bug - gy When I go
trav - 'ling to the town. I like to
hear old Dob - bin's clip - clap, I like to
feel the wheels go 'round.

Sing In Two Parts

When you know the song well, sing the chorus and verse as **partner songs.**
Group 1 sings the chorus. Group 2 sings the verse.
Change parts for verse 2.

* Start verse here.

DO-RE-MI

Rote Song

Music by Richard Rodgers/Lyrics by Oscar Hammerstein

D: d' s m d
1 2 1 sing

D
Doe . . . a deer, a fe - male deer,
A7
Ray . . . a drop of gold - en sun.
D
Me . . . a name I call my - self,
A7
Far . . . a long, long way to run,
D G
Sew . . . a nee - dle pull - ing thread,

E A
La . . . a note to fol - low sew,
F♯ Bm
Tea . . . a drink with jam and bread, That will
G A7 D
bring us back to doe!
D
Do - re - mi - fa - so - la - ti - do!

Find the notes for the scale in the last line on the staff and on the **modulator**. Touch them as you sing the line.

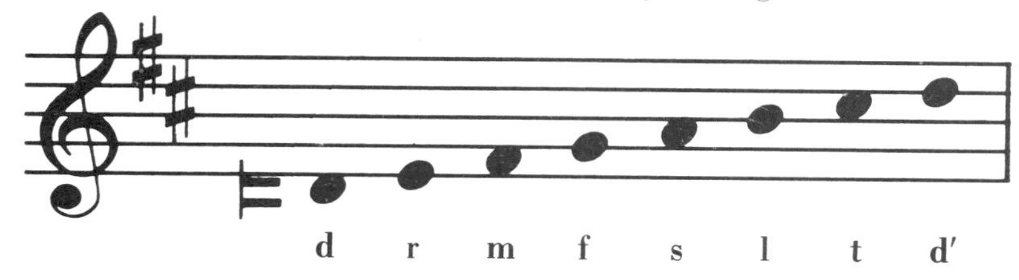
d r m f s l t d′

Modulator

d′
t
l
s
f
m
r
d

THE MARVELLOUS TOY

Rote Song

Tom Paxton

E : d' s m d m s
1 2 3 4 1 2 sing

E♭
B♭7
1. When I was just a wee lit - tle lad
2. The first time that I picked it ___ up, I

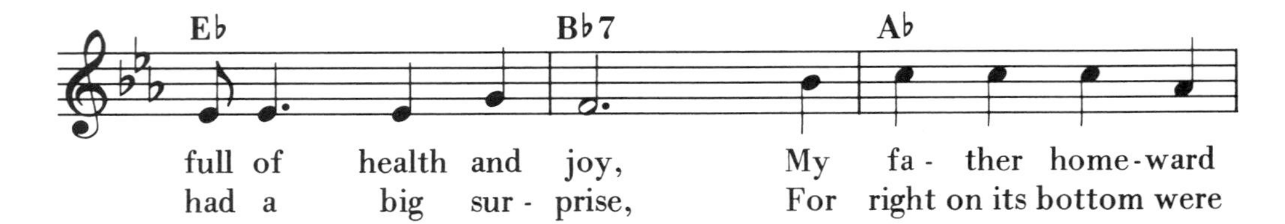

E♭
B♭7
A♭
full of health and joy, My fa - ther home-ward
had a big sur - prise, For right on its bottom were

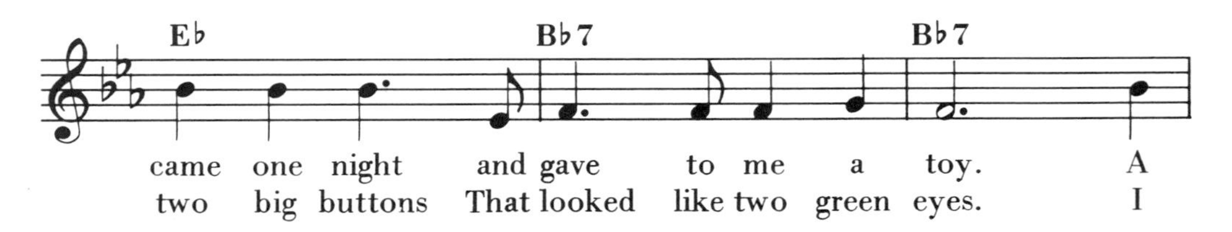

E♭
B♭7
B♭7
came one night and gave to me a toy. A
two big buttons That looked like two green eyes. I

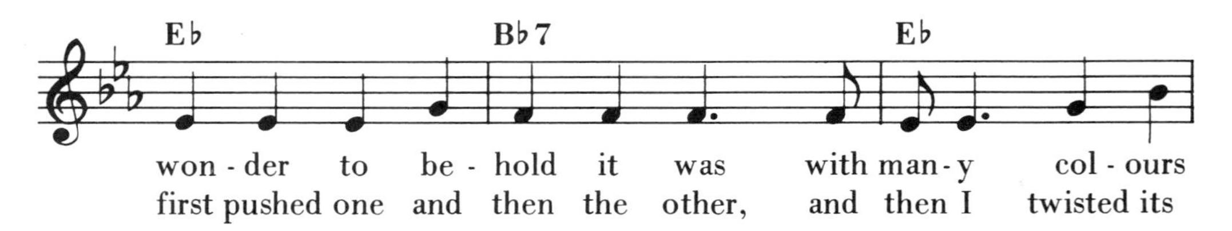

E♭
B♭7
E♭
won - der to be - hold it was with man - y col - ours
first pushed one and then the other, and then I twisted its

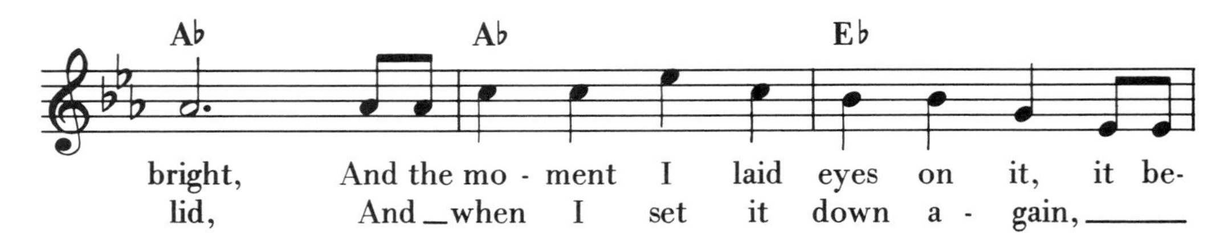

A♭
A♭
E♭
bright, And the mo - ment I laid eyes on it, it be-
lid, And _ when I set it down a - gain, ___

Bb7
Bb7
Chorus
Eb
came my heart's de - light.
here is what it did:
It went "Zip" when it moved and
Bb7
Eb
Ab
"Bop" when it stopped, and "Whirr" when it stood still, I
Ab
Eb
Bb7
Eb
nev - er knew just what it was, and I guess I nev - er will.

3. It first marched left and then
marched right
and then marched under a chair,
And when I looked where it had gone
it wasn't even there!
I started to sob and my daddy laughed
for he knew that I would find,
When I turned around my marvellous toy
would be chuggin' from behind.

4. Well the years have gone by too quickly,
it seems,
and I have my own little boy,
And yesterday I gave to him
my marv'lous little toy.
His eyes nearly popped right out of his head
and he gave a squeal of glee.
Neither one of us knows just what it is
but he loves it just like me.

What sound effects could you use for the words "zip," "bop," and "whirr?"

BIFFY

Note Song

C: d′ s m d
1 2 1 sing

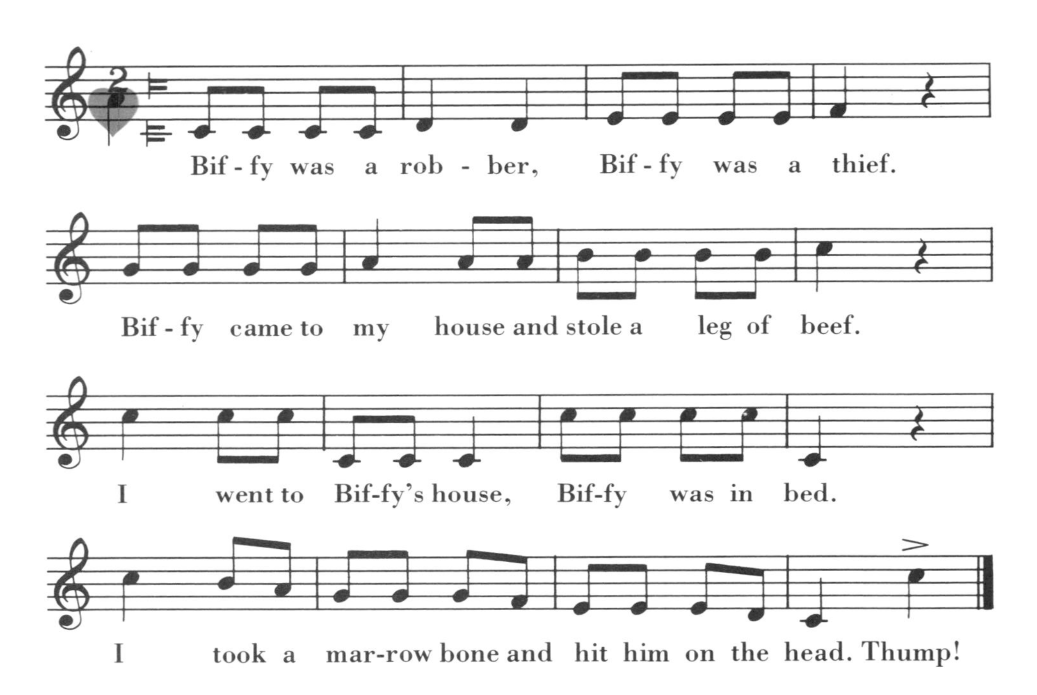

Bif - fy was a rob - ber, Bif - fy was a thief.
Bif - fy came to my house and stole a leg of beef.
I went to Bif-fy's house, Bif-fy was in bed.
I took a mar-row bone and hit him on the head. Thump!

Play the xylophone from left to right.
What happens to the sound of the notes?
What scale does this make?

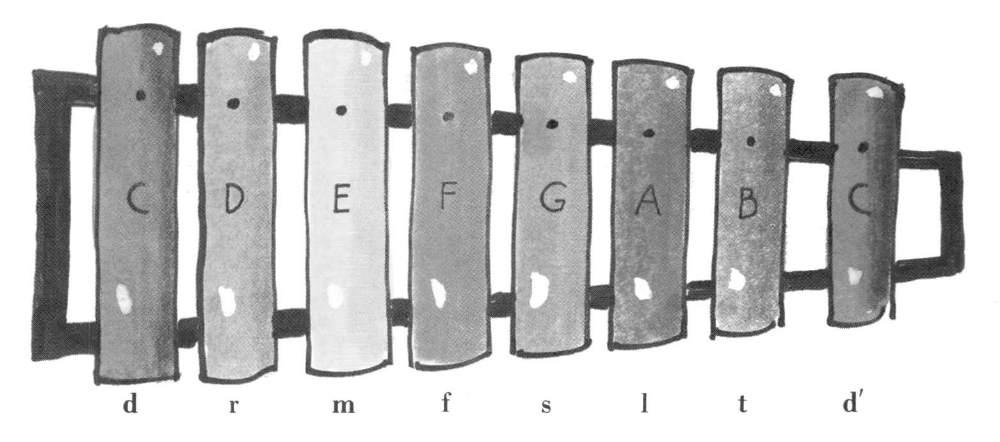

C D E F G A B C
d r m f s l t d′

Play "Biffy" on the xylophone.

WINTER

THE SHEPHERD BOY

Rote Song

M. Greenfield

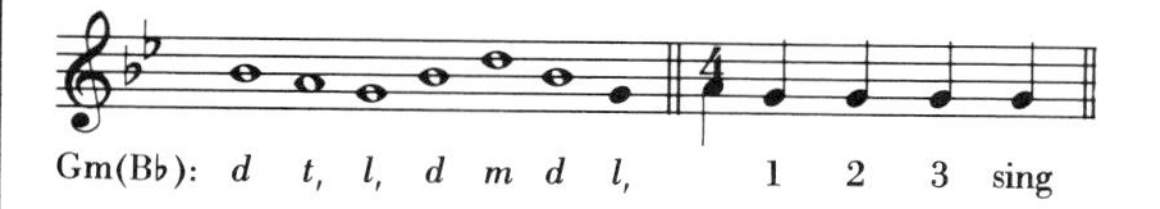
Gm(B♭): d t, l, d m d l,
1 2 3 sing

▬ Shows two **silent beats.**
Listen for the stillness of this magic night as you feel the beats.

Gm D Gm D

1. *Mary:* "Who comes knock-ing, knock-ing at the door?

Gm Cm Gm Cm Gm

Jo - seph, please, will you go?" *Joseph:* "Who comes knock-ing?

Cm D7 Gm D7 Gm

Just a lit - tle boy, Cold and wet with snow."

Gm D Gm D

2. *Boy:* "I come knock-ing, knock-ing at the door.
3. *Mary:* "Bless you shep-herd, for the lit - tle lamb.

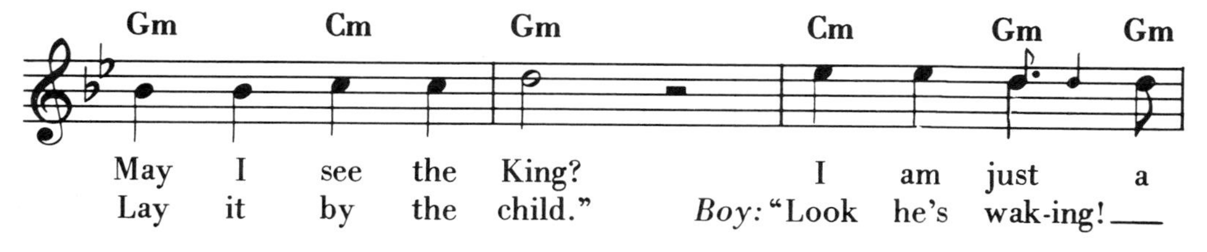
Gm Cm Gm Cm Gm Gm

May I see the King? I am just a
Lay it by the child." *Boy:* "Look he's wak-ing! ___

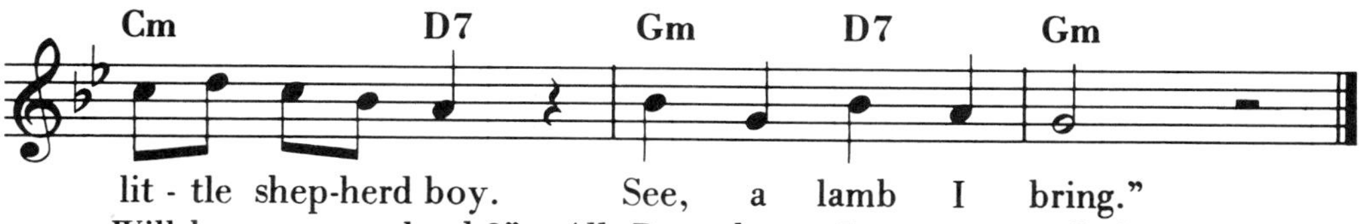
Cm D7 Gm D7 Gm

lit - tle shep-herd boy. See, a lamb I bring."
Will he see my lamb?" *All:* Ba - by Je - sus smiled.

BIRTHDAY PRESENTS

Note/Rote Song

Japanese Folk Melody/Lyrics by E.L. Thomas

D: d' s m d m s
1 2 1 sing

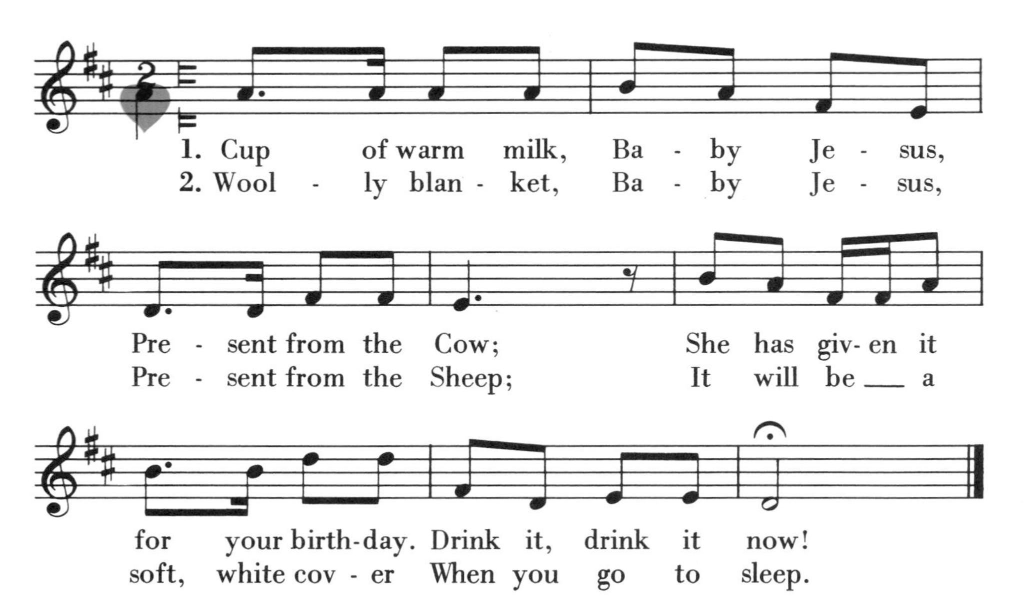

1. Cup of warm milk, Ba - by Je - sus,
2. Wool - ly blan - ket, Ba - by Je - sus,
Pre - sent from the Cow; She has giv- en it
Pre - sent from the Sheep; It will be ___ a
for your birth-day. Drink it, drink it now!
soft, white cov - er When you go to sleep.

3. If you're hungry, Baby Jesus,
What will you eat then?
Taste this brown egg, you will like it,
Brought by mother hen.

4. Here's another present, Jesus,
When you want some fun.
On his back the colt will take you
Riding in the sun.

An **ostinato** is a pattern that's repeated over and over again.

Sing or play an **ostinato** to accompany the song.
Listen to the melody to know when
to sing the last word.

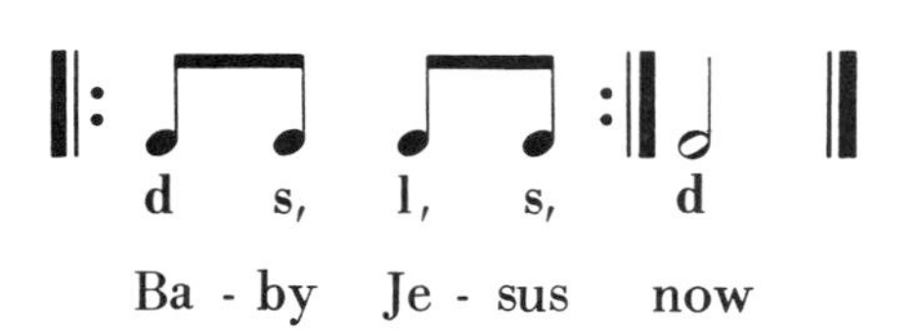

d s, l, s, d
Ba - by Je - sus now

JOY TO THE WORLD

Note/Rote Song

G.F. Handel

D: d' s m d m s d'
1 2 1 sing
f D
A 7 D
1. Joy to the world, the Lord is come!
2. Joy to the world, the Sav - iour reigns!
G A7 D
Let Earth re - ceive her King.
Let men their songs em - ploy.
mf D
Let ev - 'ry heart Pre - pare Him room
While fields and floods, Rocks, hills and plains
p D mf A7
And heav'n and na - ture sing, And heav'n and na - ture sing,
Re - peat the sound-ing joy, Re - peat the sound-ing joy,
f D D A7 D
And heav'n, and heav'n and na - ture sing.
Re - peat, re - peat the sound - ing joy.

Use this scale pattern as an introduction and ending for the song:

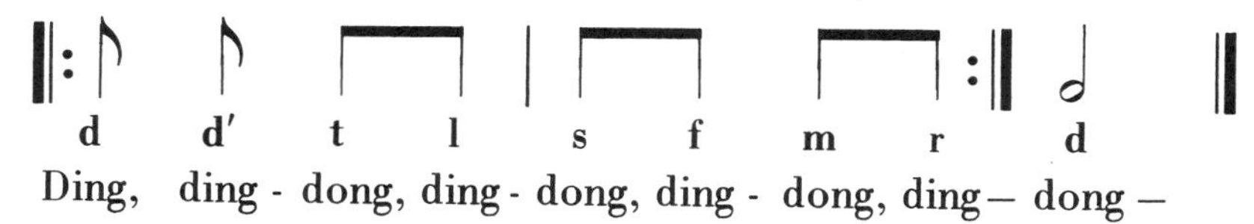
d d' t l s f m r d
Ding, ding - dong, ding - dong, ding - dong, ding — dong —

Play it on bells or tone bars, or sing it to imitate bells.

NUTTIN' FOR CHRISTMAS

Rote Song

S. Tepper and R. Bennett

G: d m s m d s,
1 2 3 4 1 2 sing

BE A DETECTIVE:
Find the words of the verse
which are sung to this pattern.
What happens to the sound of the pattern?
f
m
r
d

G C G G D7 G

1. I broke my bat on John-ny's head, Some-bo-dy snitch'd on me.
2. I put a tack on teach-er's chair, Some-bo-dy snitch'd on me.
3. I won't be see-ing San- ta Claus, Some-bo-dy snitch'd on me.

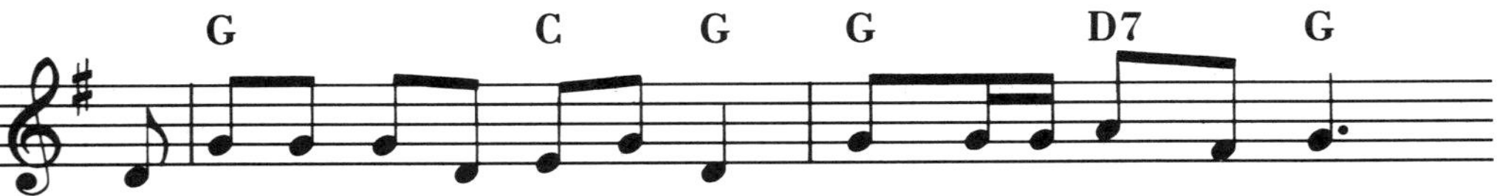
G C G G D7 G

I hid my frog in sis -ter's bed, Some - bo-dy snitch'd on me.
I tied a knot in Suz - ie's hair, Some - bo-dy snitch'd on me.
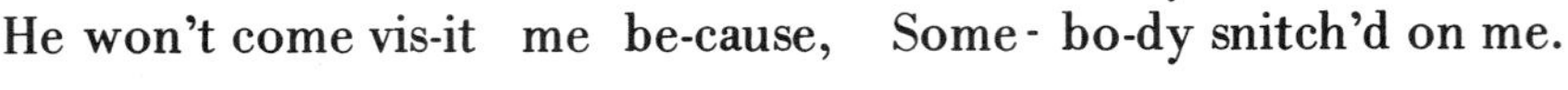
He won't come vis-it me be-cause, Some - bo-dy snitch'd on me.

G C D7 G

I spill'd some ink on Mom-my's rug, I made Tom-my eat a bug,
I did a dance on Mom-my's plants, Climbed a tree and tore my pants,
Next year I'll be go-ing straight, Next year I'll be good, just wait!

G Am D G
Bought some gum with a pen-ny slug. Some-bo-dy snitch'd on me. Oh,
Filled the su - gar bowl with ants. Some-bo-dy snitch'd on me. Oh,
I'd start now, but it's too late. Some-bo-dy snitch'd on me. Oh
Chorus
G
I'm get - tin' nut - tin' for Christ - mas,
D7
Mom - my and dad - dy are mad.
G
I'm get - tin' nut - tin' for Christ - mas,
D7 G
'Cause I ain't been nut - tin' but bad!

JOLLY OLD ST. NICHOLAS

Composer Unknown

Note/Rote Song

A: d m s m d m
1 2 1 sing

A
E7
A

1. Jol - ly Old St. Nich - o - las, Lean your ear this way,
2. When the clock is strik-ing twelve, When I'm fast a - sleep,
3. John - ny wants a choo-choo train, Su - sie wants a sled,

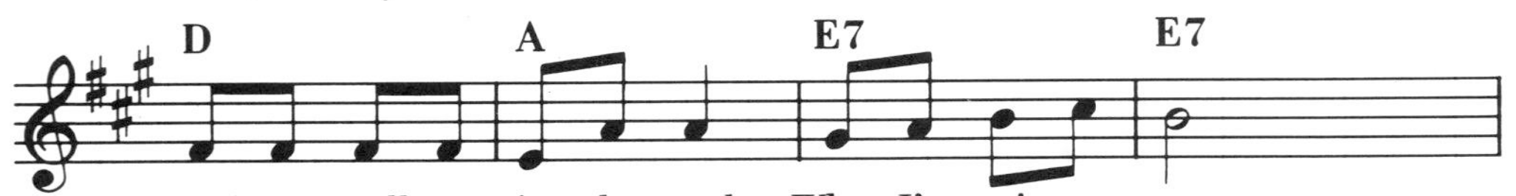
D
A
E7
E7

Don't you tell a sin - gle soul What I'm going to say.
Down the nar - row chim - ney flue With your pack you'll creep.
Nel - ly wants a box of paints, Yel - low, blue and red.

A
E7
A
A

Christ-mas Eve is com - ing soon, Now, you dear old man,
Soon you'll find the stock-ings there Hang-ing in a row,
Now I think I'll leave to you What to give the rest.

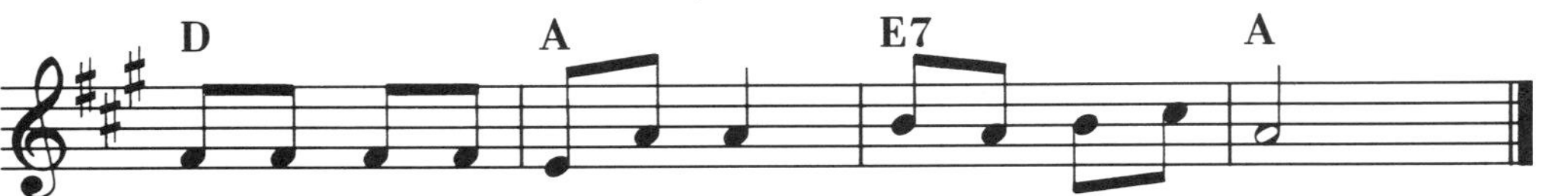
D
A
E7
A

Whis-per what you'll bring to me, Tell me if you can.
Mine will be the short-est one, Mend-ed at the toe.
Choose for me, dear San - ta Claus, You will know the best.

BE A DETECTIVE:

Which lines or **phrases** use only **mi, re,** and **doh?** Sing them using handsigns.

JINGLE BELLS

Note/Rote Song

J. Pierpont

G: d m s m d s,
1 2 3 sing

Dashing through the snow
In a one-horse open sleigh.
O'er the fields we go,
Laughing all the way.
Bells on bob-tail ring,
Making spirits bright.
What fun it is to ride and sing
A sleighing song tonight. Oh –

Chorus Jingle bells, jingle bells,
Jingle all the way.
Oh, what fun it is to ride
In a one-horse open sleigh! **(Repeat)**

Accompany the song.
Add a jingle bell **ostinato** to the verse:

Sing, or play this on tone bars, during the chorus:

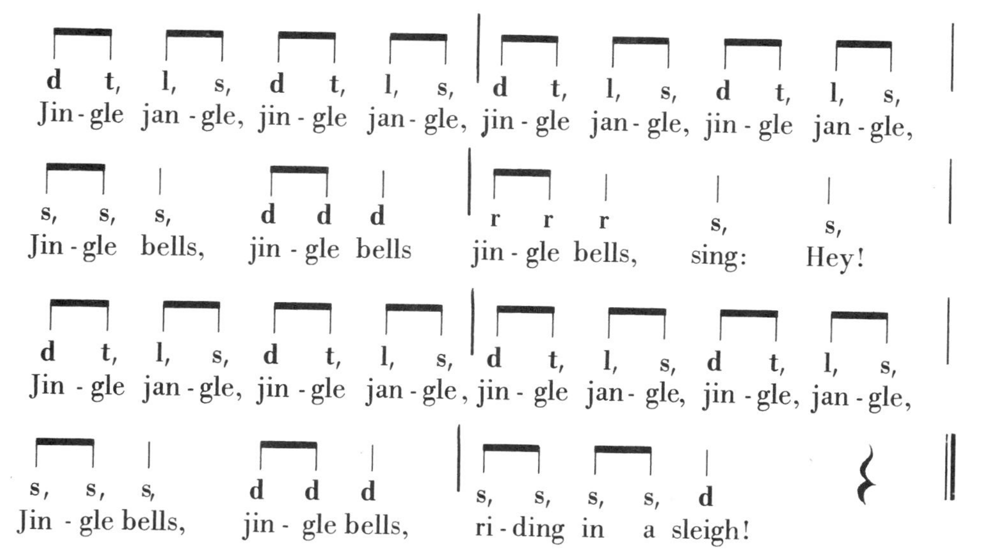
d t, l, s, d t, l, s, d t, l, s, d t, l, s,
Jin-gle jan-gle, jin-gle jan-gle, jin-gle jan-gle, jin-gle jan-gle,
s, s, s, d d d r r r s, s,
Jin-gle bells, jin-gle bells jin-gle bells, sing: Hey!
d t, l, s, d t, l, s, d t, l, s, d t, l, s,
Jin-gle jan-gle, jin-gle jan-gle, jin-gle jan-gle, jin-gle, jan-gle,
s, s, s, d d d s, s, s, s, d
Jin-gle bells, jin-gle bells, ri-ding in a sleigh!

PIÑATA

Rote Song

Mexican Folk Song

D: d' s m d m s
1 2 1 sing

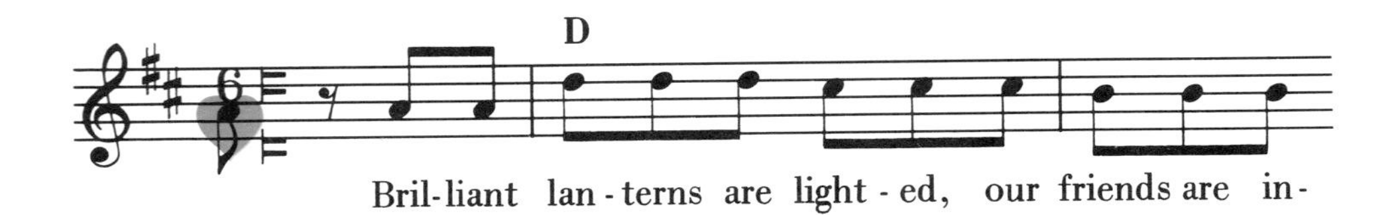

D
Bril-liant lan-terns are light-ed, our friends are in-

A7
vit-ed, in cho-rus u-ni-ted, "Pi-ña-ta!"

There's no need to re-mind us, with blind-folds they'll

D
bind us, they'll turn and they'll wind us "Pi-ña-ta!"

D
Ay, que bue-na, Ay, que bue-na,

A7
D
Ay, que bue-na, que bue-na, que bue-na.

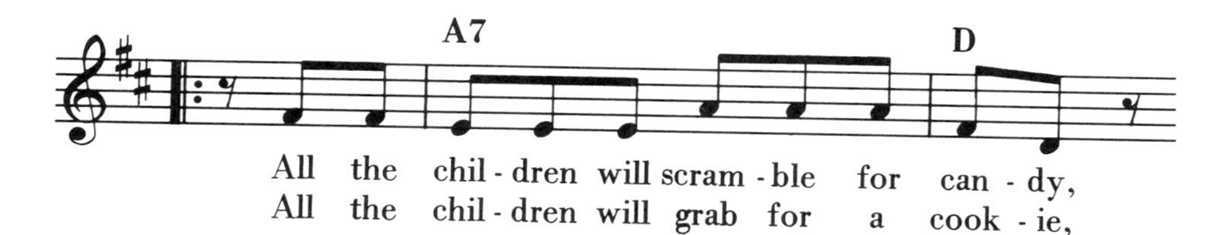
A7
D
All the chil - dren will scram - ble for can - dy,
All the chil - dren will grab for a cook - ie,

A7
D
All the chil - dren will scram-ble and shout.
And the oth - er good things that spill out.

In Mexico, Christmas Eve parties always have a *piñata* for the children. It is a decorated clay bowl or bag, filled with candies and hung from the ceiling. The children, blind-folded, take turns trying to break it with a large stick.

CHILDREN, GO WHERE I SEND THEE

Rote Song

American Folk Song

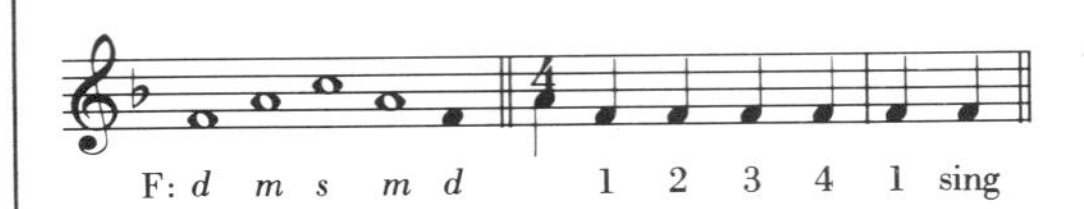
F: d m s m d
1 2 3 4 1 sing

Chil-dren, go where I send thee; How shall I
send thee? I will send thee { one by one, two by two, } Well,
1. One was the lit-tle bit-ty ba - by, Wrapped in swad-dling
2. Two was the Paul and Si - las, (repeat 1)
cloth - ing, Ly - ing in a man - ger.
Born, born, oh, Born in Beth-le-hem.

3. Three was the three men riding . . .
4. Four was the four come a-knockin' at the door . . .
5. Five was the gospel preachers . . .
6. Six was the six who couldn't get fixed . . .
7. Seven was the seven who went to heaven . . .
8. Eight was the eight who stood by the gate . . .
9. Nine was the nine who saw the sign . . .
10. Ten was the ten commandments . . .

SONG OF THE CRIB

Note/Rote Song

German

F: d m s m d m s
1 2 1 sing

1. Jo - seph dear - est Jo - seph mine,
2. I will glad - ly, la - dy mine,

Help me rock the child di - vine.
Help thee rock the child di - vine.

God re - ward both thee and thine, In
God's pure light on thee will shine, In

par - a - dise, So prays the moth - er
par - a - dise, So prays the moth - er

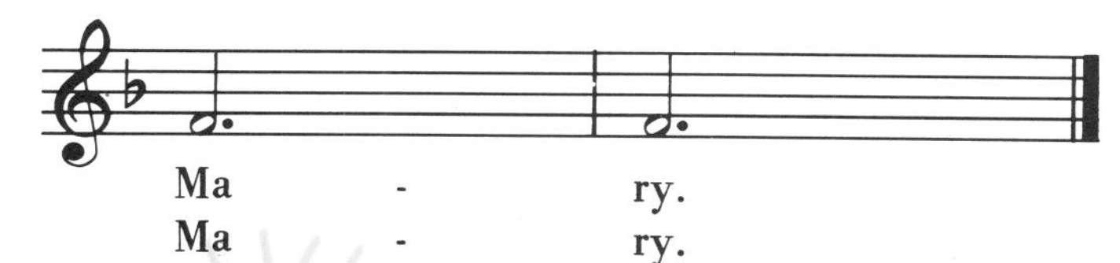
Ma - ry.
Ma - ry.

3. Softly as the stars do shine,
Gently rock the child divine,
Heaven's joy is yours and mine,
In paradise,
So prays the mother Mary.

The baby is rocked by **soh, mi** and **doh** in this carol.
Find **s - m - d** in the music.

IT'S CHRISTMAS

Rote Song

Dorothy Lees-Blakey

D: d' s m d m s f
1 2 3 4 1 2 sing

1. It's Christ-mas! It's Christ-mas! San - ta Claus is
2. The babe in the man-ger, Love for ev - 'ry
com - ing! Can't you hear the sleigh bells in the
stran- ger, Mes - sa-ges of peace and hope a -
night? It's snow - ing, it's
new. Young car - ol - lers
snow - ing! Win - ter winds are blow - ing,
call - ing, As the snow is fall - ing,
Soon there'll be a ma - gic world of white.
Mer - ry, mer - ry Christ-mas time to you!

I'M SUPER, I'M SMART

Rote Song

Music by L. Fowler / Lyrics by E. Stenson

C: d' t l s d' s d'
1 2 3 sing

Feel the silent beats.
Snap your fingers on the rests.

Chorus
C F C
Well I'm su - per, I'm smart, I'm as good as can be. There's
F G7
some - thing aw - ful - ly nice a - bout me, most of the
1. 2.
C E7 Am G
time. But some-times,
3.
C
time.
Verse
C F C
1. Well I get gum in my hair, and I get dirt on my face, and I
F G7
have my clothes all o - 'er the place, I put my el - bows on the ta - ble and I
D.C.
talk when I eat, but most of the time, I'm kind - a neat.

2. Well, I spill my milk and I track up the floor,
And I'm late for dinner and I slam the door,
I forget to say please, and I fall off my seat,
But most of the time I'm kinda neat . . .

3. Well my room's a mess and I don't feed the cat,
And I rip my jeans and then I loose my hat,
And I leave my toys out on the street,
But most of the time I'm kinda neat . . .

LOHRI

Rote Song

East Indian Chant

The Festival of Lohri marks the end of winter in India. On January 13th, Indian children celebrate by gathering treats from neighbours. Afterwards, everyone in the community sits around a fire, singing songs and eating nuts.

A: d l, s, l, d l,
1 2 3 sing

Sun-dar Mun-dar-i e Ho Ter-a kon wi-char-a Ho
Fine
Du-la Bha-thi wa-la Ho Du-le dhe vei-a-e Ho
Gur e sha-kar pa-ie Ho Gur di-yah ra-ri a Nee, Bha-
Spoken
(2nd time no repeats)
D.C. al Fine
ra-wan Jor-i-ah Nee Pa Mai Loh-ri Jee-ve ta-ri Jo-ri

Play a passing game:
Pass a treat around a circle.

x means to pick up the treat from in front of you.
o means to pass the treat to your neighbour on the left.

BASSEZ DOWN

Rote Song

West Indian Folk Song

D: d' s m d m s d'
1 2 1 sing

D
A7
D
Bas - sez, ma-ma, bas - sez down.
A7
D
D
A7
Bas-sez in the morn-in', bas-sez down. Bas - sez, ma-ma,
D
A7
D
Fine
bas-sez down. Bas-sez in the morn-in', bas-sez down.
D
A7
Bas-sez down, Mis-sie Ma-ry, bas-sez down. Bas - sez
A7
D
D
down, Mis-sie Ma-ry, bas-sez down. Bas-sez down Mis-sie Ma-ry,
G
A7
D
D.C. al Fine
bas-sez down. Bas-sez in the morn-in', bas-sez down.

For boys' names sing "Miste' " instead of "Missie."

PERCUSSION INSTRUMENTS

Percussion instruments are musical instruments
that are hit, shaken or scraped.
They are used to keep the beat, perform rhythms, or create special effects.

bongos
guiro
sleigh bells
tambourine
maracas
sand blocks
triangle

Which instruments make hitting sounds?
shaking sounds?
scraping sounds?
Which instrument makes two kinds of sounds?
What other percussion instruments can you name?

Sing "Bassez Down" on page 59.
Play the steady beat on percussion instruments.
Choose one kind of sound for the chorus, and
a different kind of sound for the verse.

LISTENING:

"Sleighride": A German Dance

Wolfgang Mozart

When Mozart was alive over 200 years ago, there were no radios, record players or tape recorders. When people wanted to dance, a composer had to write music for an orchestra to play.

Wolfgang Mozart wrote many dances.
In this one, he used several melodies.

How many times can you hear this **melody**?
Sing it when you hear it.

Listen for the sleighbell section.

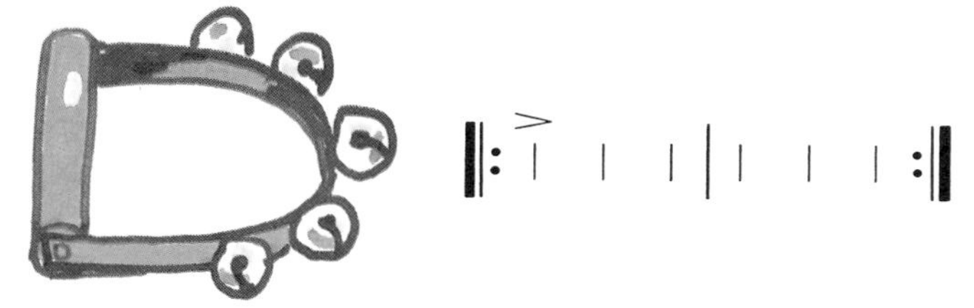

Listen for the trumpet playing **octave** jumps.

octave

Now, divide into two groups.
Everyone sings the melody when it is heard.
Group 1 shake imaginary sleighbells when they hear them.
Group 2 draw the trumpet's octave jumps in the air when they hear them.
Switch parts.

MUSIC MATH

DIVIDING THE BEAT

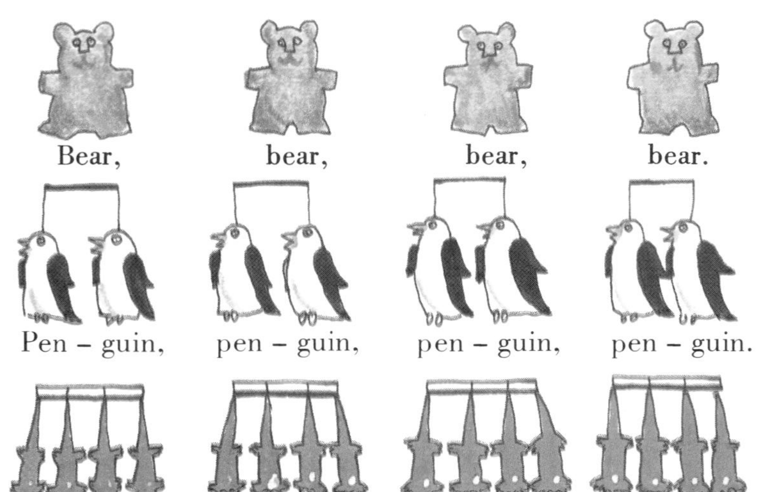

Bear, bear, bear, bear.

Pen – guin, pen – guin, pen – guin, pen – guin.

Sal - a - man - der, sal - a - man - der, sal - a - man - der, sal - a - man - der.

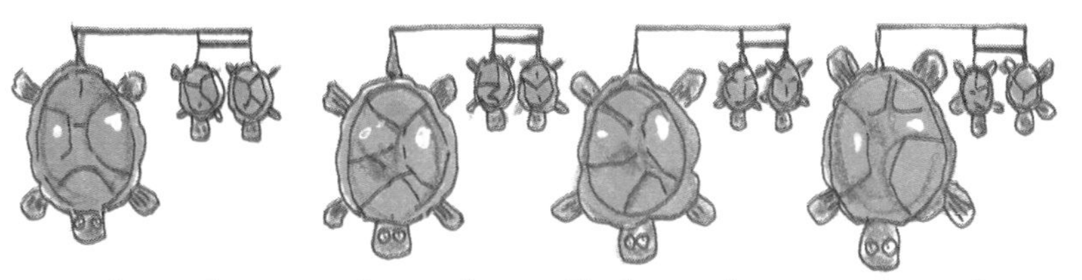

Mud tur-tle, mud tur-tle, Mud tur-tle, mud tur-tle.

METRIC MUSIC MEASURES UP

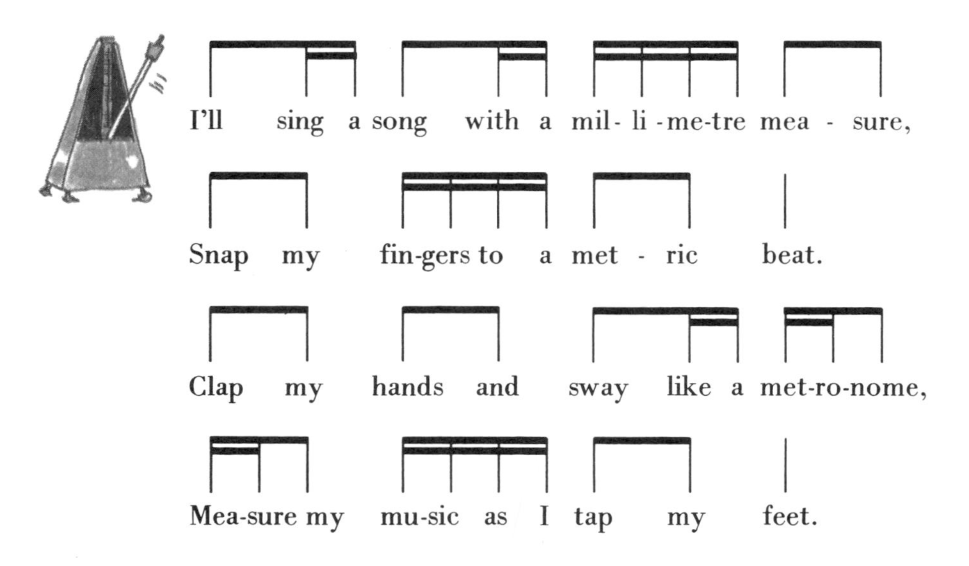

I'll sing a song with a mil- li -me-tre mea - sure,

Snap my fin-gers to a met - ric beat.

Clap my hands and sway like a met-ro-nome,

Mea-sure my mu-sic as I tap my feet.

COMPOSE YOUR OWN RHYTHM PIECE

Clap these rhythm phrases.
Feel the steady beat inside you.

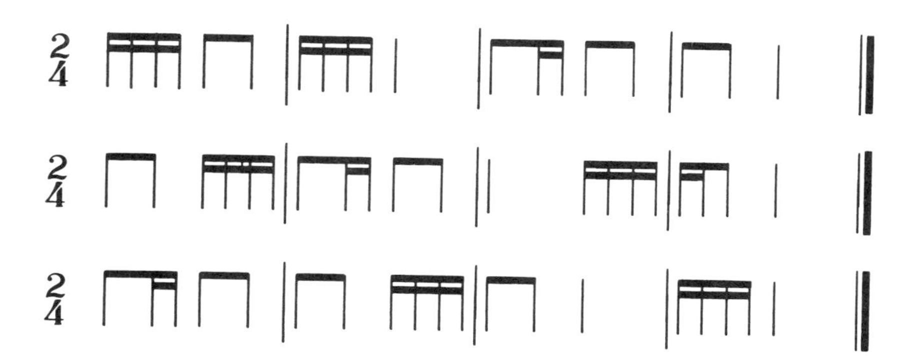

2/4
2/4
2/4

Songs and other kinds of music are composed by putting sections of music in a certain order.
Choose two sections from above to make an ABA piece.
Write your piece down.
Perform your rhythm piece using a different percussion instrument for each different section.

FRERE JACQUES

Note Song and Round

Traditional

F: d m s m d
1 2 1 sing

1. *Frè - re Jac- ques, Frè - re Jac- ques,*
2. Are you sleep - ing? Are you sleep - ing?

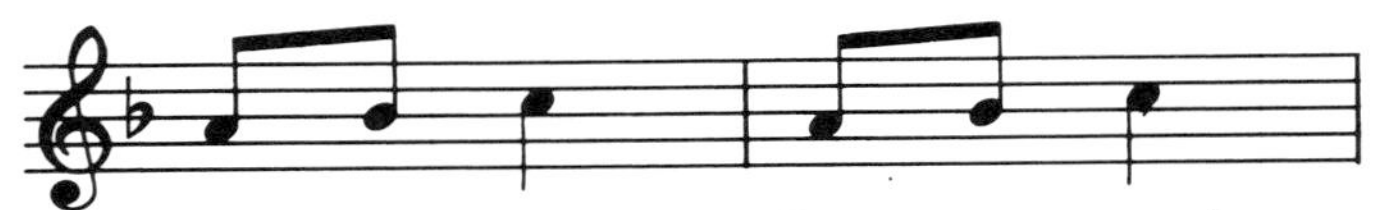

Dor - mez vous? Dor - mez vous?
Bro - ther John, Bro - ther John?

Son-nez les ma - tin - es! Son-nez les ma - tin - es!
Morn-ing bells are ring - ing. Morn-ing bells are ring - ing.

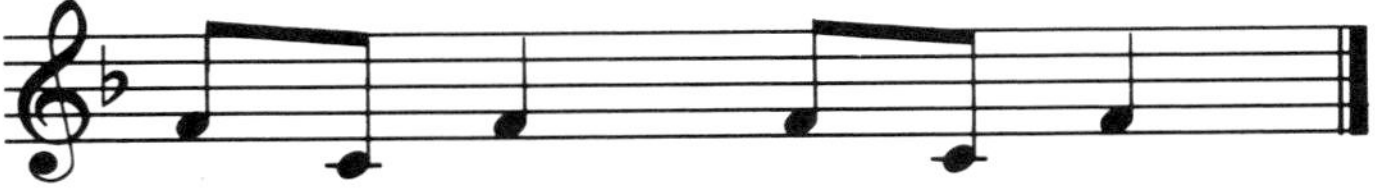

Din, din, don. Din, din, don.
Ding, ding, dong. Ding, ding, dong.

DIVIDING THE BEAT

Clap an ostinato as you sing the song:

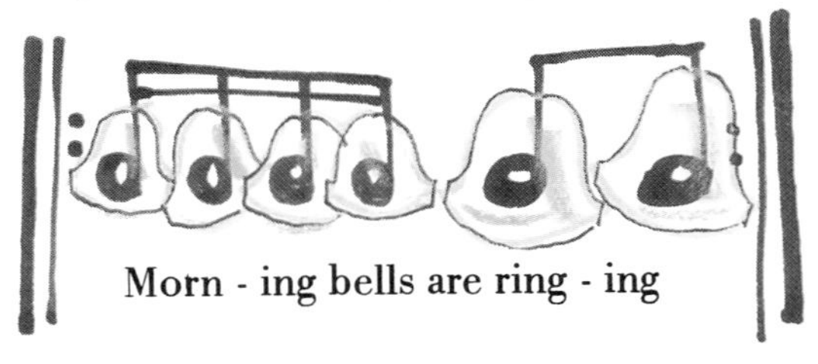
Morn - ing bells are ring - ing

This song moves in twos.
Conduct it like this:

THREE BLIND MICE

Note Song

Traditional

F: d m s m
1 2 1 sing

Three blind mice. Three blind mice. See how they run!

See how they run! Oh, my, how they fly! Oh, my, how they fly!

Three blind mice. Three blind mice.

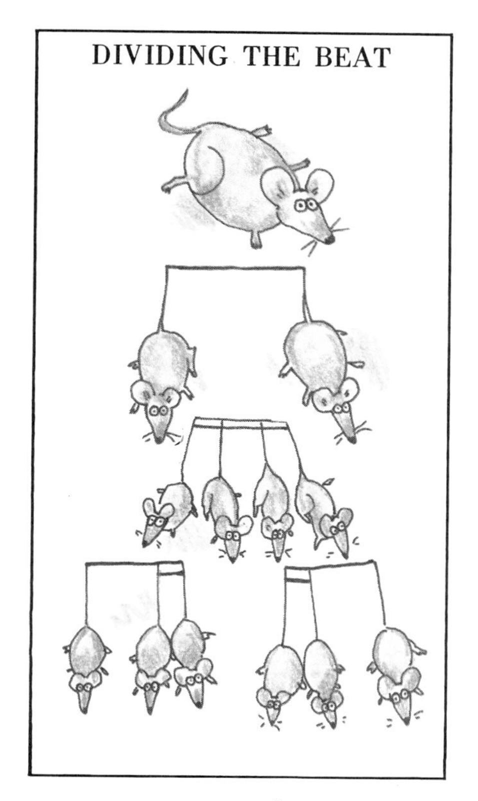
DIVIDING THE BEAT

Clap this rhythm as you sing the song.

Oh, my, how they fly!

"Three Blind Mice" and "Frère Jacques" are **partner songs**. When you know both songs well, sing them together.

C-C-C-C-COLD

Note/Rote Song

Danish Melody/Lyrics by John Wood

G: d m s m d s,
1 2 1 sing

G
D7

1. There was a man and he did sing,
A - cross the north land it would ring,

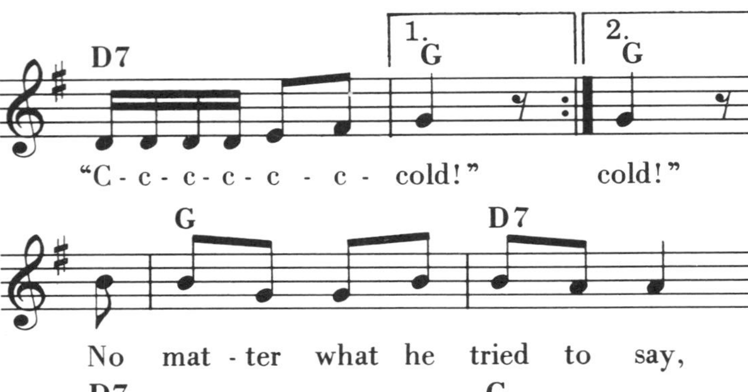

D7
1. G
2. G
"C - c - c - c - c - c - cold!" cold!"
G
D7
No mat - ter what he tried to say,

D7 G

"C - c - c - c - c - c - c - c," night or day,

C
G

His words kept com - ing out this way,

D7
G

"C - c - c - c - c - c - cold!"
"C - c - c - c - c - c - cold!"

𝄾 is a silent ♪. Touching your nose quickly will help you feel the shortness of the silence.

2. The little man was very thin
"C-c-c-c-c-c-cold!"
With icy whiskers on his chin,
"C-c-c-c-c-c-cold!"

One night he had an awful dream,
"C-c-c-c-c-c-c-c," he did scream,
"For my dessert don't serve ice-cream
C-c-c-c-c-c-cold!"

THE TIE

A tie joins two notes together.
Sing the first note and hold it through the second.
How many beats will you hold the tied notes?
What bar has a tie in the next song?

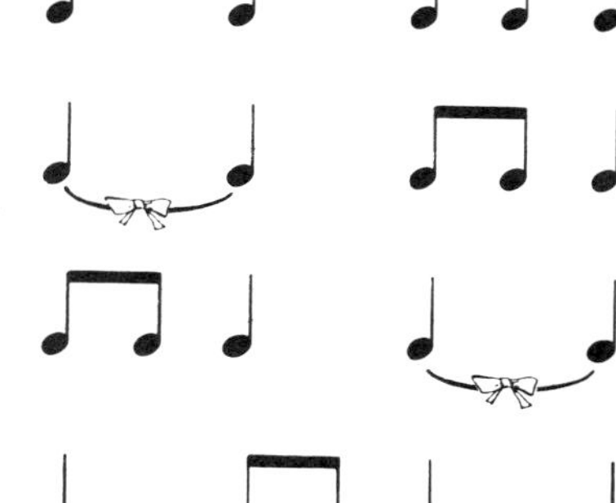

TOUT CELA EST A MOI

Rote Song

Renée Durand

G: d m s m
1 2 1 sing

1. Un nez, deux yeux. Un nez, deux yeux.
One nose, two eyes. One nose, two eyes.

Chorus
Tout, tout, tout, tout, tout, tout, tout, tout, Tout ce-la est à moi.

2. *Une bouche, deux oreilles.* (repeat verse 1) (mouth, ears)
3. *Une tête, deux mains.* (repeat verses 2, 1) (head, hands)
4. *Un cou, deux bras.* (etc.) (neck, arms)
5. *Une poitrine, deux épaules.* (chest, shoulders)
6. *Un dos, deux jambes.* (back, legs)
7. *Un ventre, deux pieds.* (tummy, feet)

SKIP TO MY LOU

Note/Rote Song

American

G: d m s m d m
1 2 1 sing

Jumping 3rds

Our voice jumps a 3rd when we skip a note. Find these **skips** in the song

1. Flies in the but-ter-milk, shoo, fly, shoo.
Flies in the but- ter-milk, shoo, fly, shoo.
Flies in the but-ter-milk, shoo, fly, shoo.
Skip to my Lou, my dar - ling.
Chorus
Lou, Lou, skip to my Lou. Lou, Lou, skip to my Lou.
Lou, Lou, skip, ______ skip. Lou, Lou, skip, ______ skip.
Lou, Lou, skip to my Lou, Skip to my Lou, my dar - ling.
Lou, Lou, skip, ___ skip. Skip to my Lou, my dar - ling.
s f m r d
m r d
f m r d t,
r d t,

2. Lost my partner, what'll I do? . . .
3. I'll find another one, prettier 'n you. . .

VALENTINE SONG

Rote Song

Mary Trotter

Eb: d' s m d m s
1 2 3 sing
Eb Ab Eb
1. Val-en-tine, Val-en-tine, you're look-in' fine!
2. Val-en-tine, Val-en-tine, I want to say:
Eb Bb7
Val-en-tine, Val-en-tine, say you'll be mine.
"Val-en-tine, Val-en-tine, have a great day!"
Chorus
Ab Eb Bb7
How I love your hap-py face! How I love your smile!
Eb7 Ab Bb7 Eb
How I'd like to take you home to stay with me a-while.

TONY CHESTNUT

Note Song

Game Song

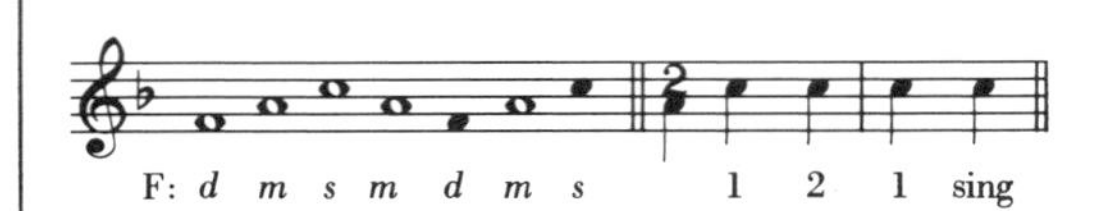
F: d m s m d m s
1 2 1 sing

To - ny Chest - nut knows I love you,
To - ny knows, To - ny knows. To - ny Chest- nut
knows I love you, That's what To - ny knows.

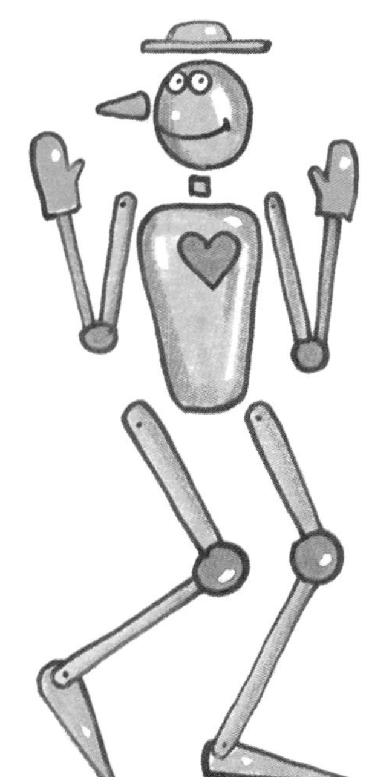

Play this game:
Touch a body part for each syllable.

To - toes		I - eyes	
ny - knees		love - heart	
chest - chest		you - point to a friend	
nut - head		that's - clap hands	
knows - nose		what - clap hands	

How are the **beats** grouped in the song?

or

How can you tell by looking at the music?
How would you conduct the song?

THE WILD OAK TREE

Rote Song

Traditional

D: d' s m d 1 2 1 sing
D G D
Love grows un-der the wild oak tree,
A7 D A7
Su - gar melts like can - dy.
D A G D
Top of the moun - tain shines like gold, And you
D A7 D Fine
kiss your lit - tle fell - a sort - a han - dy.
G D A7 D
Dreams, dreams, sweet dreams, Un-der the wild oak tree.
G D A7 D D.C. al Fine
Dreams, dreams, sweet dreams, One for you and one for me. Oh,

SAME, ALMOST THE SAME, DIFFERENT

Find hats that are
the same
almost the same
different.

Musical ideas can also be
the same
almost the same
different.

MY HAT

Note/Rote Song

German Folk Song

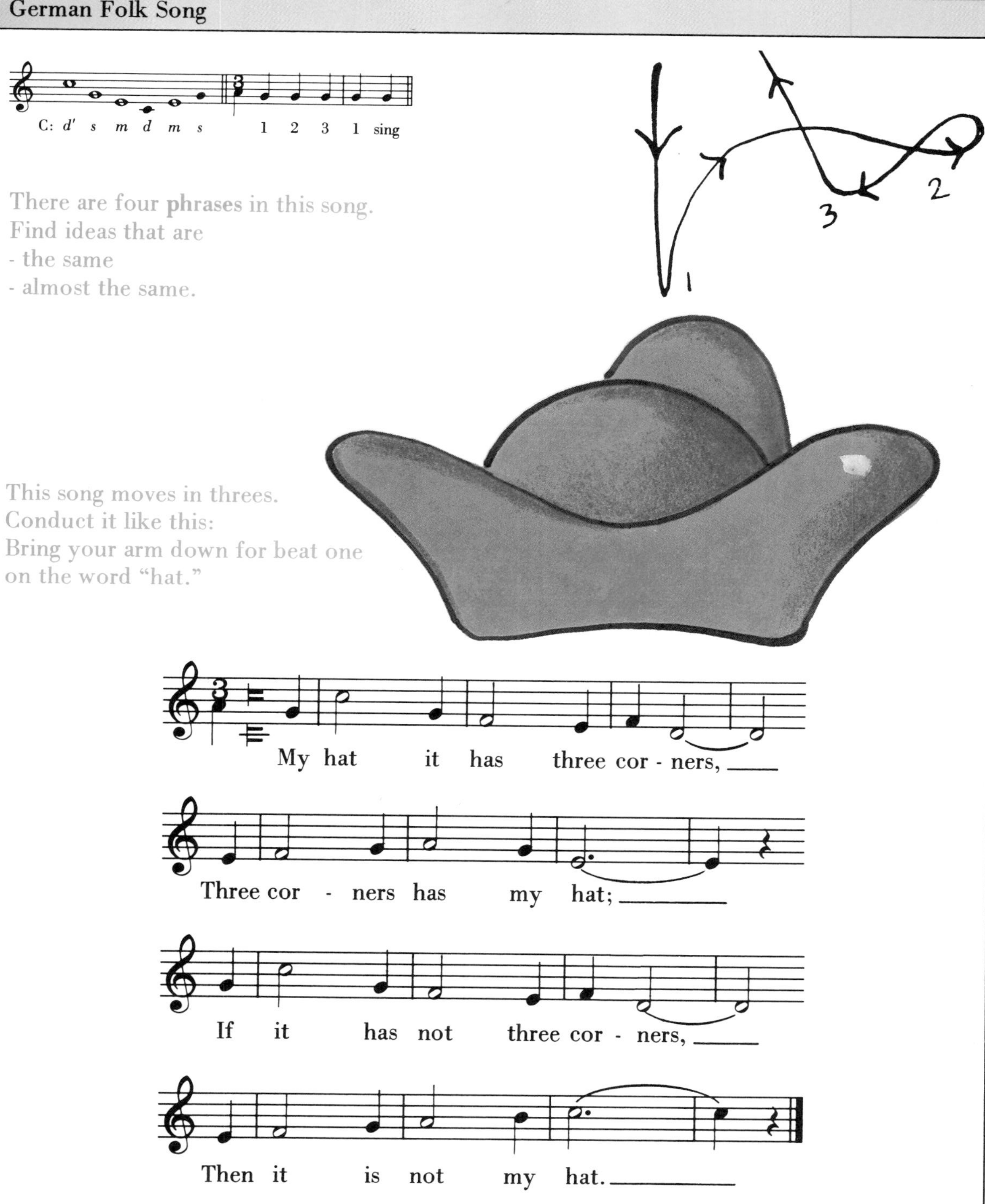
C: d' s m d m s
1 2 3 1 sing
1
2
3
My hat it has three cor - ners,
Three cor - ners has my hat;
If it has not three cor - ners,
Then it is not my hat.

There are four **phrases** in this song.
Find ideas that are
- the same
- almost the same.

This song moves in threes.
Conduct it like this:
Bring your arm down for beat one on the word "hat."

CHIAPANECAS

Note Song

Mexican Dance/Lyrics by L. MacDowell and M. Trotter

G: d m s m d
1 2 3 1 2 sing

(clap, clap)
1. 'Way down in old Mex - i - co, o - lé!
Chorus: Oh! Chia - pa - ne - cas, o - lé, o - lé!
(clap, clap)
That is where I'd like to go, o - lé!
Oh! Chia - pa - ne - cas, o - lé, o - lé!
(clap, clap)
They dance and clap as they play, o - lé!
Oh! Chia - pa - ne - cas, o - lé! o - lé!
(clap, clap)
Ev - 'ry - one does it this way, o - lé!
Oh! Chia - pa - ne - cas, o - lé! o - lé!

2. Ev'ryone join in the fun, *o-lé*!
Come dance and clap in the sun, *o-lé*!
Swing to the left and the right, *o-lé*!
Jump up with all of your might, *o-lé*!

Notice how phrase one skips up and down by 3rds.
Find a phrase exactly like phrase one.
What do you notice about the other two phrases?

MAGIC PENNY

Rote Song

Malvina Reynolds

Eb: d' s m d s, d
1 2 3 sing

Eb
Eb
Love is some-thing if you give it a - way,
Bb 7
Eb
Eb
Give it a - way, Give it a - way, Love is some-thing if you
Eb
Bb 7
Eb
Fine
give it a - way, You end up hav-ing more.
Ab
Eb
Bb 7
It's just like a ma - gic pen-ny, Hold it tight and you
Eb
Ab
won't have an - y. Lend it, spend it, and you'll
Eb
Bb 7
D.C. al Fine
have so man-y, They'll roll all o - ver the floor, for

STAND TALL

Posture Chant

M. Trotter

Stand tall—when you sing
you gotta stand up tall!
Stand tall—when you sing
you gotta give your all!
Spread your feet, just a little,
put your weight on your toes,
Make one straight line
right up to your nose.
Don't slouch like a grouch,
you don't live in a pail,
Lift your chest—tuck your tummy—
then tuck your tail!
Put your hands by your side
and wear a great big smile:
Stand tall when you sing,
Now—you got style!

I WON'T GET UP

Rote Song

Katherine Davis

E♭: d' s m d m s
1 2 3 1 sing

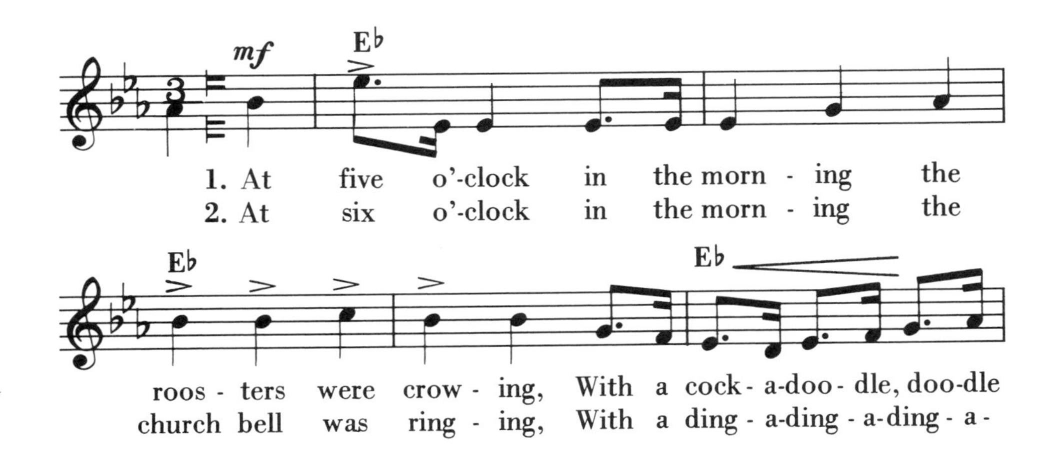

mf
E♭
1. At five o'-clock in the morn - ing the
2. At six o'-clock in the morn - ing the
E♭
E♭
roos - ters were crow - ing, With a cock - a-doo - dle, doo-dle
church bell was ring - ing, With a ding - a-ding - a-ding - a -

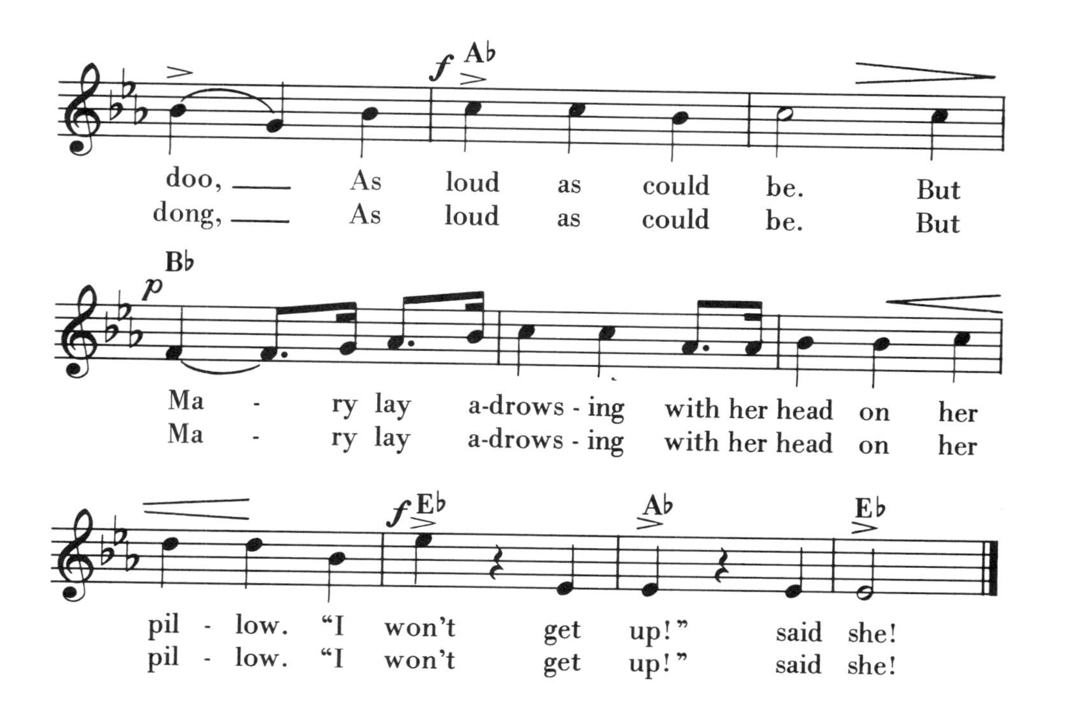
Ab
Bb
p
Eb
Ab
Eb
doo, — As loud as could be. But
dong, — As loud as could be. But
Ma - ry lay a-drows - ing with her head on her
Ma - ry lay a-drows - ing with her head on her
pil - low. "I won't get up!" said she!
pil - low. "I won't get up!" said she!

3. At sev'n o'clock in the morning
Her mother was calling
With a "Mary, Mary, Mary, Mary"
As loud as could be.
But Mary lay adrowsing
With her head on her pillow.
"I won't get up!" said she.

4. At eight o'clock in the morning
The breakfast was cooking,
You could smell the coffee and the bacon
As plain as could be.
Then Mary left her pillow
With a speed most surprising.
"And now I'm up!" said she.

This song has markings which will help you tell the story of the song.

>	*accent* — sing the note a little louder.
p	*piano* — soft
mf	*mezzo forte* — medium loud
f	*forte* — loud
<	*crescendo* — gradually louder
>	*diminuendo* — gradually softer

THE TOTTENHAM TOAD

Note Song

English Cumulative Song/Additional Lyrics by C. Winter

B : d m d s,
1 2 3 4 1 2 sing

B♭
B♭

1. The Tot-ten-ham toad came trot-ting up the road, With his
2. The Bir-ming-ham bat, he tipped his lit-tle hat, With his

B♭
F7
B♭

feet all swim-ming in the sea. *Sau-cy lit-tle squirr'l with her*
el - bow rest-ing on his knee. *La-zy lit-tle lynx, she just*

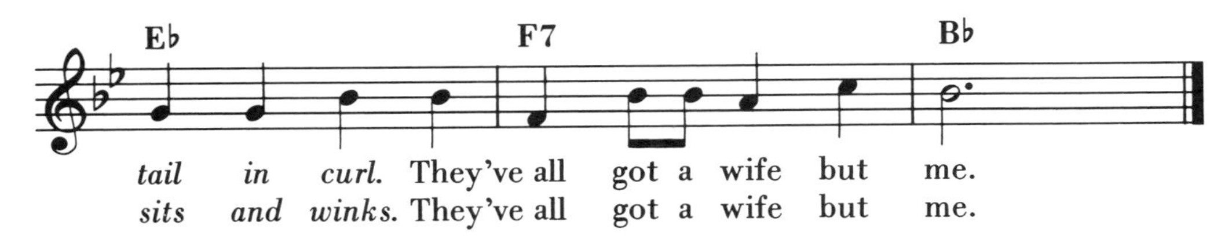

E♭
F7
B♭

tail in curl. They've all got a wife but me.
sits and winks. They've all got a wife but me.

Jump down ↓ a 4th
↑
↓
s, d d s,
Jump up ↑ a 4th

BE A DETECTIVE:

How many 4th jumps can you find?
going up?
going down?

3. The Wimbledon whale, he stood upon his tail,
As he ate three cups of bread and tea.
Dimpled little dog, in her hollow log.
They've all got a wife but me.

4. The Canterbury crow said, "Now I've got to go.
It's so sad, it fills me full of glee!"
Friendly little fly, with her apron high.
They've all got a wife but me.

5. The Galloway goat, he buttoned up his coat,
As he climbed the branches of a tree.
Busy little bird, she is feather'd, not furred.
They've all got a wife but me.

MAORI STICK GAME

Rote Song

New Zealand

F: d m s m d m s
1 2 3 1 2 sing

Mah - koo - oh Koh - teh - ah weh Koo-ee tah - nah,
Mah- koo - oh Koh - teh - ah weh Koo-ee tah - nah.

Lummi sticks are used by Maori natives to accompany their chants.
Use this **ostinato** as you sing:

floor together out

LUMMI STICKS

Make your own lummi sticks.
Cut an old broom handle into two pieces, each 25 cm long.
Paint 12 cm of each stick with your favourite colour. The coloured end will be the bottom of the stick.

25 cm
12 cm

Try new ways of working with your lummi sticks:

- Find new ways to strike the sticks.
- Make up new patterns.
- Work with a partner.

SCOTLAND'S BURNING

Note Song and Round

Traditional

G: d m s m d s,
1 2 1 sing

1
2
Scot-land's burn-ing, Scot-land's burn-ing. Look out! Look out!

Fire! Fire! Fire! Fire! Pour on wa - ter, Pour on wa - ter.

BE A DETECTIVE:
How are these two songs different?
How are they the same?

FIRE'S BURNING

Note Song and Round

Traditional

G: d m s m d s,
1 2 3 1 sing

1
2
Fire's burn - ing, Fire's burn - ing. Draw near - er, Draw near - er.

In the gloam-ing, In the gloam-ing, Come sing and be mer - ry.

WORKING WITH A PARTNER

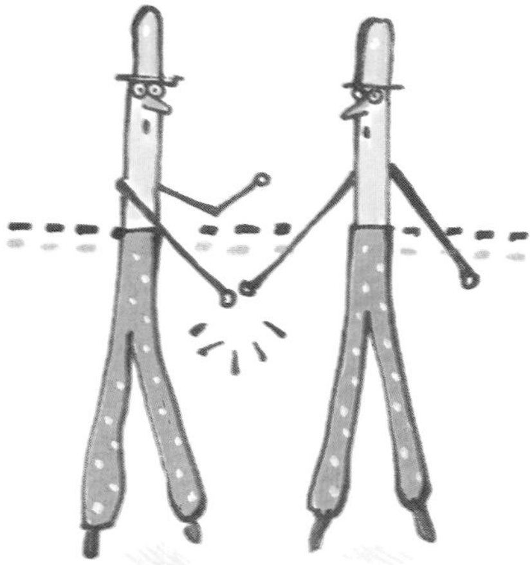

Scot - land's burn - ing Look out!
soh, soh, doh doh re mi

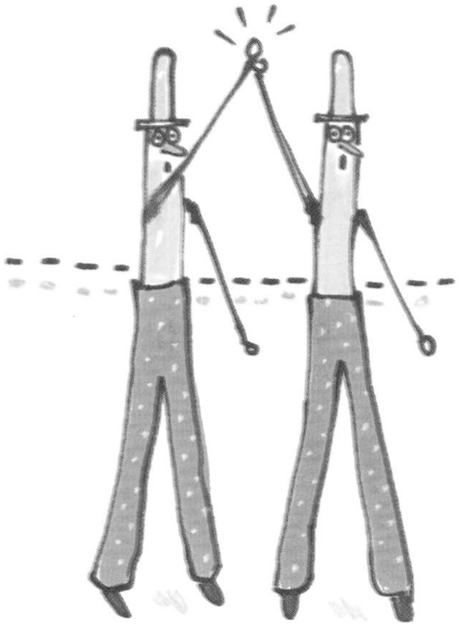

Fire! Fire! Pour on wa - ter.
soh soh soh, soh, doh doh.

Add actions to the song "Scotland's Burning."
Do the actions alone. Do them with a partner.

ART HAS EXPRESSION TOO

Art uses **colour, shape** and **line** to set a mood or tell a story.
What does this picture tell you?

THE MUDDY PUDDLE

I am sitting
In the middle
Of a rather Muddy
Puddle
With my bottom
Full of bubbles
And my rubbers
Full of Mud.

While my jacket
And my sweater
Go on slowly
Getting wetter
As I very
Slowly settle
To the Bottom
Of the Mud.

And I find that
What a person
With a puddle
Round his middle
Thinks of mostly
In the muddle
Is the Muddi-
Ness of Mud.

Dennis Lee

'NEATH THE LILACS

Rote Song

Action Song

C: d s m d m s
1 2 3 1 sing

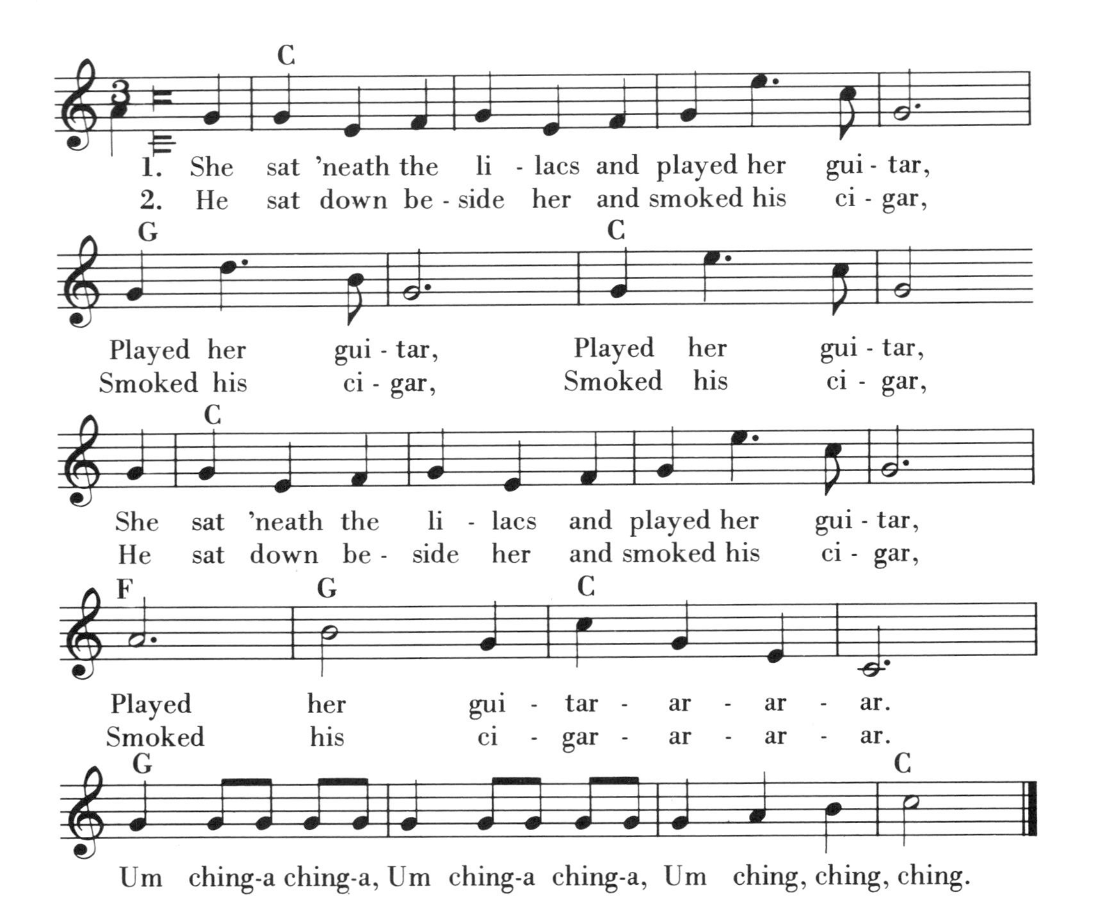

C
1. She sat 'neath the li - lacs and played her gui - tar,
2. He sat down be - side her and smoked his ci - gar,
G
C
Played her gui - tar, Played her gui - tar,
Smoked his ci - gar, Smoked his ci - gar,
C
She sat 'neath the li - lacs and played her gui - tar,
He sat down be - side her and smoked his ci - gar,
F
G
C
Played her gui - tar - ar - ar - ar.
Smoked his ci - gar - ar - ar - ar.
G
C
Um ching-a ching-a, Um ching-a ching-a, Um ching, ching, ching.

3. He said that he loved her but oh, how he lied . . .
4. She said she believed him but oh, how she sighed . . .
5. They were to be married but she up and died . . .
6. He went to her funeral but just for the ride . . .
7. He sat on her tombstone and laughed till he died . . .
8. She went to heaven and flip-flap she flied . . .
9. He went the other way and frizzled and fried . . .
10. The moral of this story is: Don't tell a lie . . .
11. Or you too may perish and frizzle and fry . . .

MORE PERCUSSION INSTRUMENTS

These percussion instruments can play melodies as well as beats and rhythms.
What action must you use to make them sound?

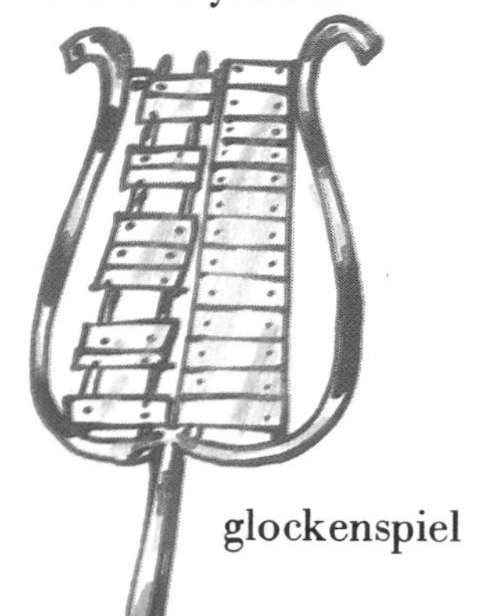

glockenspiel

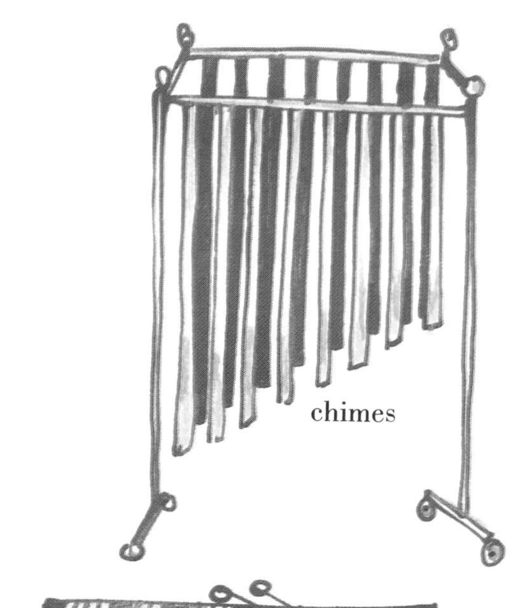

chimes

timpani

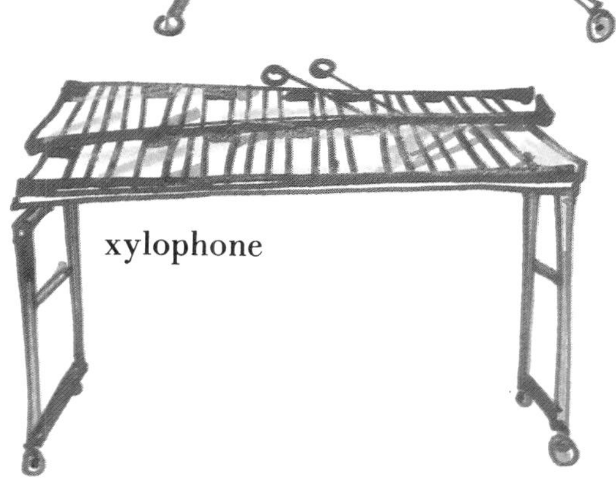

xylophone

Here are some mallets used for striking percussion instruments.

hard-headed mallets

wooden mallet

felt-covered mallets

Which would you choose to make
– soft, gentle sounds?
– hard, crisp sounds?

SUGAR SHACK RAMBLE

START
HERE
WHOA!
SHSHSH
BLP
BLP
GEE UP!

Tell the SUGAR SHACK RAMBLE story with sounds.

* How will you make the horses sound closer and closer to the sugar shack?
* How will they sound as they move away?

MAPLE SYRUP

Note Song

Gordon Fleming

F: d m s m d m s
1 2 3 sing

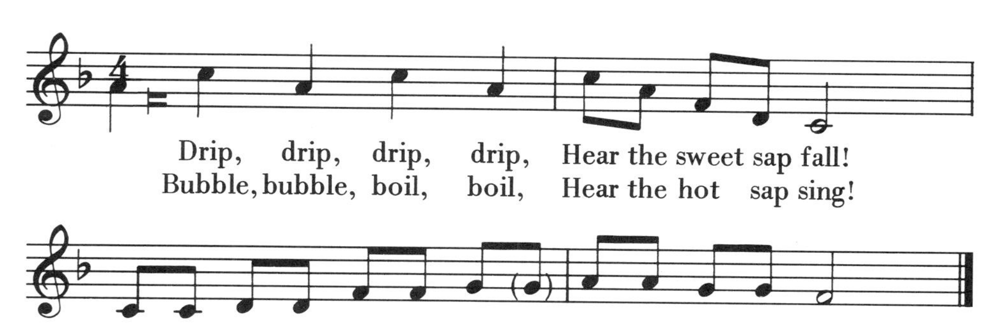
Drip, drip, drip, drip, Hear the sweet sap fall!
Bubble, bubble, boil, boil, Hear the hot sap sing!
Bring me ket-tles! Bring me pails! Hear the farm-ers call.
Soon we'll have a dain-ty dish to set be-fore the King.

Sing or play these **ostinato** patterns on a xylophone or glockenspiel.

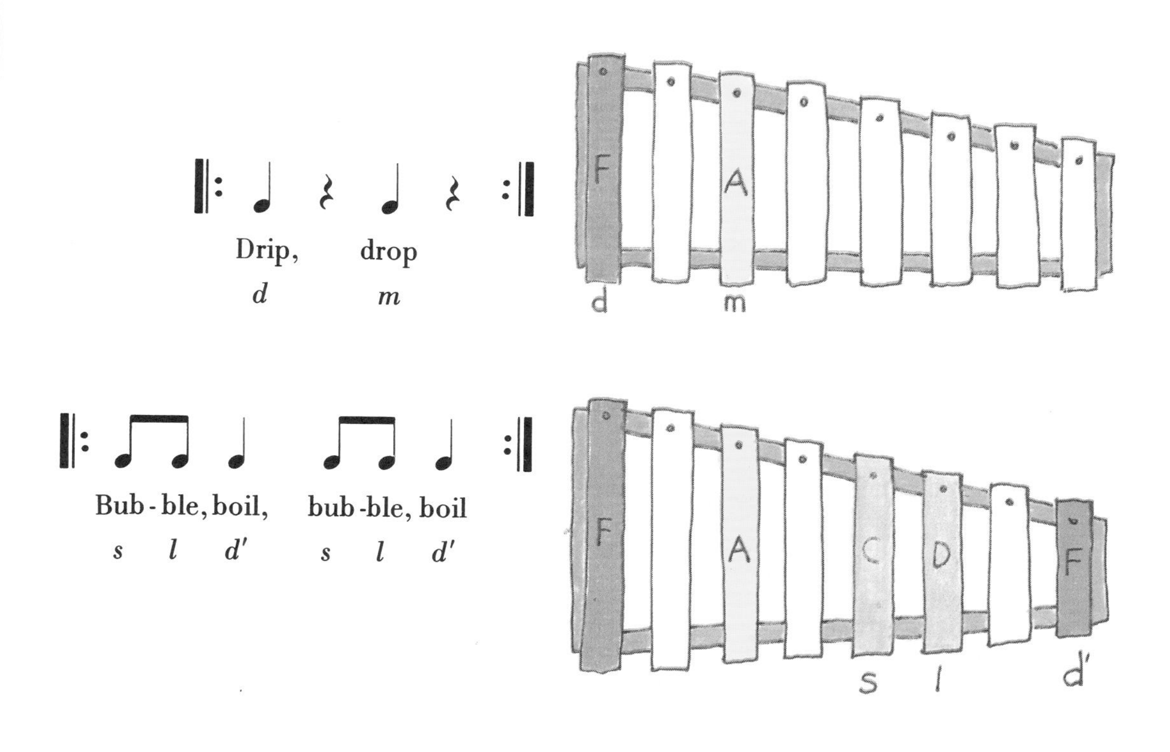
Drip, drop
d m
F
A
d m
Bub-ble, boil, bub-ble, boil
s l d' s l d'
F
A
C
D
F
s l d'

MARCH OF THE LEPRECHAUNS

Rote Song

Irish

G: d m s m d s,
1 2 1 sing

G G
1. The lep - re-chauns are march-ing, They're march-ing through the
2. The lep - re-chauns are march-ing, I think it's three by
D D
hall. They're march- ing on the ceil - ing, They're
three. Just close your eyes and try now to
D7 G G
march - ing on the wall. They're march - ing two by
vis - ual - ize with me. Their mer - ry lit - tle
G D
two, And now it's four by four. You
feet will nev - er miss a beat. They're
D D7 G
say you still can't see them. Move back, here come some more.
ve - ry trick - y fel-lows. Look out! They're un- der the sheet!

BE A DETECTIVE:

Which phrases skip **3rds** using **doh, mi** and **soh**?
Which phrases skip **3rds** using **ti, re** and **fah**?

PÉTER AND PÁL

Rote Song

Hungarian Folk Song

D: d' s m d
1 2 3 sing

1. *Haj - má - si Pé - ter, Haj - má - si Pál.*
2. Off went our Pé - ter, home stayed our Pál.

Haj - má -si Pé - ter, Haj - má - si Pál. Haj - má-si Pé - ter,
Haj - má -si (silent), Haj - má - si Pál. Haj - má-si (silent),

Haj - má-si Pál. Haj - má - si Pé - ter, Haj - ma-si Pál.
Haj - má-si Pál. Haj - má - si (silent), Haj - ma-si Pál.

3. Off went our Péter, off went our Pál.
Hajmási (silent), Hajmási (silent). (3)

4. Back came our Péter, but not our Pál.
Hajmási Péter, Hajmási (silent). (3)

5. Back came our Péter, back came our Pál.
Hajmási Péter, Hajmási Pál. (3)

Péter and *Pál* are brothers.
Their family name is *Hajmási.* (High-mah-shee)
In Hungary the family name goes
before the given name.

It's fun to play this game using hand puppets.

THE TAILOR AND THE MOUSE

Rote Song

English Folk Song

Gm (B♭): d, t, l, d m
1 2 3 4 1 2 sing

1. There was a tai - lor had a mouse, Hi did-dle un-kum fee - dle.
2. The tai-lor thought the mouse was ill; Hi did-dle un-kum fee - dle.

They lived to - geth - er in one house Hi did-dle un-kum fee - dle.
He gave him part of a blue pill, Hi did-dle un-kum fee - dle.

Chorus
Hi did-dle un-kum ta - rum tan - tum, In the town of Ram - say,

Hi did-dle un - kum, o'er the lea, Hi did-dle un - kum fee - dle.

3. The tailor thought his mouse would die . . .
He baked him in an apple pie . . .

4. The pie was cut, the mouse ran out . . .
The tailor followed him about . . .

* A weak beat before the first strong beat of a song is called a **pick-up.**

BE A DETECTIVE:

The **octaves** in this song jump from low **mi**, to high **mi.** How many octave jumps can you find?

I'M SO TIRED

Note/Rote Song

Alex Laurier

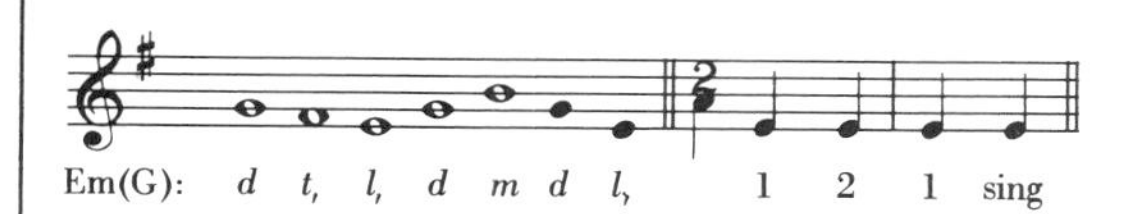
Em(G): d t, l, d m d l,
1 2 1 sing

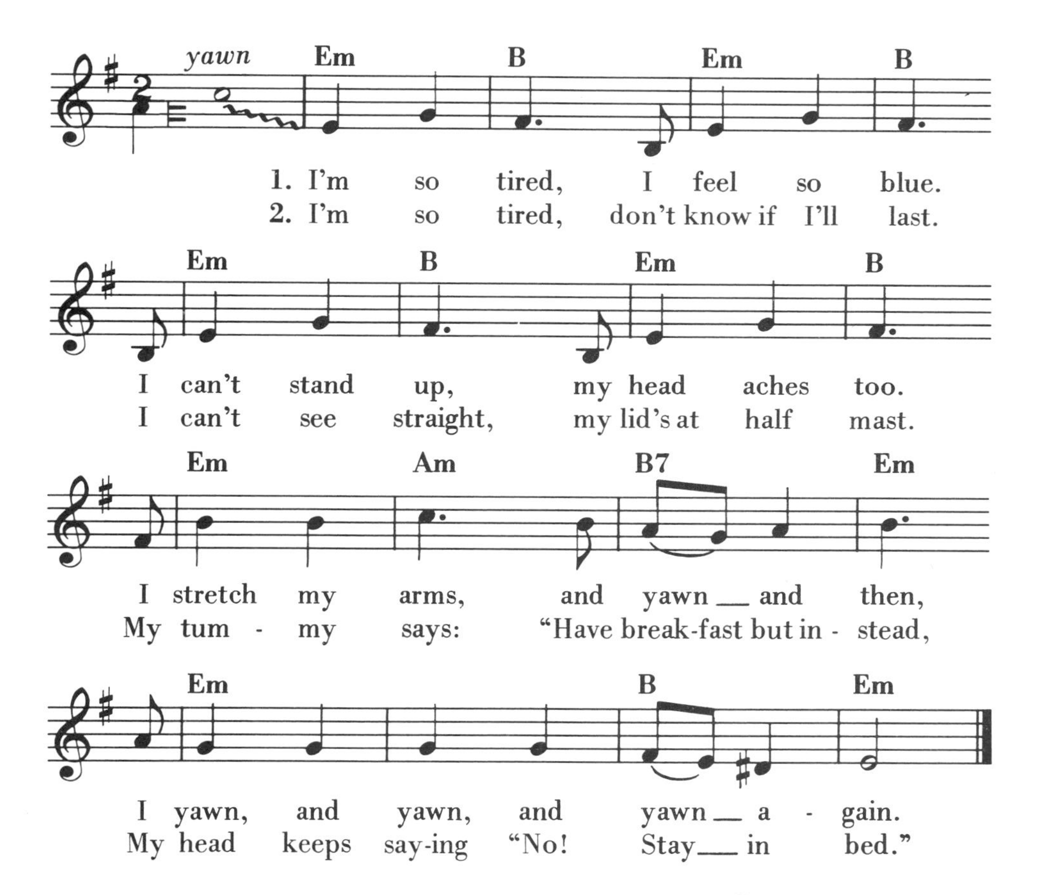
yawn
Em B Em B
1. I'm so tired, I feel so blue.
2. I'm so tired, don't know if I'll last.
Em B Em B
I can't stand up, my head aches too.
I can't see straight, my lid's at half mast.
Em Am B7 Em
I stretch my arms, and yawn — and then,
My tum - my says: "Have break-fast but in - stead,
Em B Em
I yawn, and yawn, and yawn — a - gain.
My head keeps say-ing "No! Stay — in bed."

3. I'm so tired, I fidget and squirm
I move in my bed like a wriggley worm.
No, I'm not sick, no fever, no cold.
My mom let me watch the late, late show.

4. I'm so tired, I tell no lies.
I see the world through blood-shot eyes.
And all because my mom said, "All right!"
She let me watch the late movie last night.

End verse 4 by repeating the last phrase.
Gradually slow down and sing more softly. Finish with a yawn and gentle snore.

MARY ANNE

Note Song

Dutch Melody/ English Lyrics by John Wood

G: d m s m d s, 1 2 3 1 sing

G D7 G
1. Oh! Ma - ry Anne, Ma - ry Anne, where do you go?
2. Dear Ma - ry Anne, Ma - ry Anne, what is his name?
3. My Ma - ry Anne, Ma - ry Anne, when will you wed?
G D7 G
Oh! Ma - ry Anne, Ma - ry Anne, where do you go?
Dear Ma - ry Anne, Ma - ry Anne, what is his name?
My Ma - ry Anne, Ma - ry Anne, when will you wed?
G C D7 G
I'm go - ing out with a hand - some young man.
Jon - a - than, Tim - o - thy, T - O - M, Dan.
When I'm a la - dy and when he's a man.
G D7 G
Hop - sa - sa, fa - la - la, my Ma - ry Anne.

Find the musical idea with this shape:
Where is it repeated?

Find a different musical idea:

Find one that's almost the same.
How is it different?

FINDING PATTERNS

Artists use **shapes** too—look at the painting above.

Find ideas or shapes that are the same.

Find ideas that are different.

MUSIC SHALL LIVE

Note Song and Round

German

G: d m s m
1 2 3 1 2 sing

1
All things shall per - ish un - der the sky.

2
Mu - sic a - lone shall live, Mu - sic a - lone shall live,

3
Mu - sic a - lone shall live, nev - er to die.

BE A DETECTIVE:

How many times is this pattern repeated?

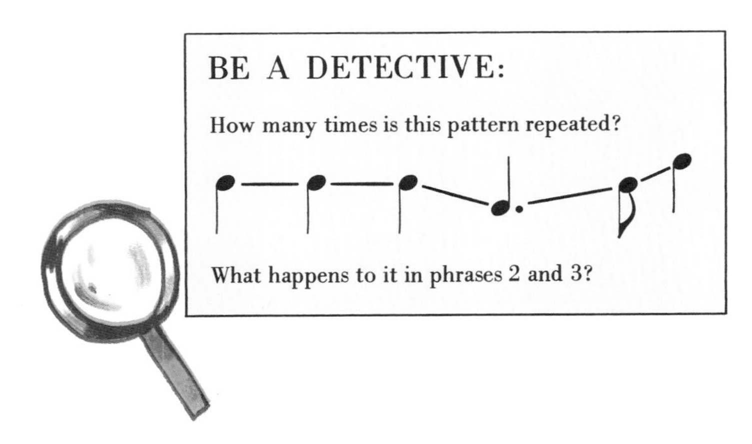

What happens to it in phrases 2 and 3?

SPRING

SARASPONDA

Note/Rote Song

Dutch Spinning Song

C: d′ s m d
1 2 3 4 1 2 sing

C G7 C
Sa - ra-spon-da, Sa - ra-spon-da, Sa - ra-spon-da, Ret- set- set!

C G7 C
Sa - ra- spon- da, Sa - ra- spon- da, Sa - ra-spon-da, Ret- set - set!

F C F C
Ah - do - ray- oh! Ah- do- ray- boom-day- oh!

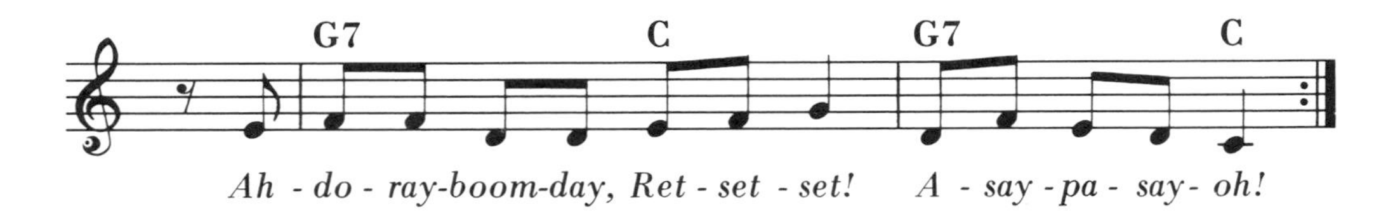

G7 C G7 C
Ah - do - ray-boom-day, Ret - set - set! A - say - pa - say- oh!

BOOM-DEE-AH-DA

Rote Song

Traditional

G: d m s m d
1 2 3 sing

G Em Am D7
1. I love the moun - tains, I love the roll - ing hills,
2. Doh loves the moun - tains, Re loves the roll - ing hills,
G Em Am D7
I love the flow - ers, I love the daf - fo - dils,
Mi loves the flow - ers, Fah loves the daf - fo - dils,
G Em Am D7
I love the fire - side when all the lights are low.
Soh loves the fire - side when all the lights are low.
Chorus
G Em Am D7
Boom dee-ah- da, Boom- dee-ah - da, Boom - dee-ah - da, Boom-dee-ah - da,
Doh - de -ah- da Lah - dee-ah - da, Re - dee-ah- da, Soh - dee-ah-da,

SING IN TWO PARTS

Divide into two groups.
Sing the chorus together as an introduction.
Group I repeats the chorus while Group II sings verse one.
Switch parts for verse two.

THE GOAT

Note/Rote Song

Traditional

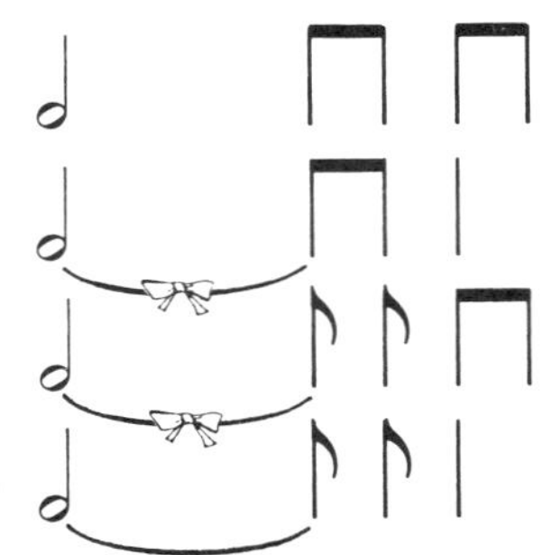

What does a tie tell you?
Find the ties in your new song.
For how many beats will you hold the tied notes?

C: d' s m d m s
1 2 3 4 1 2 sing

C
F
1. There was a man, (there was a man) now please take note, (now please, etc.)
2. One day that goat felt frisk and fine,
3. But when the train came in - to sight
G
C
There was a man who had a goat.
Ate three red shirts from off the line.
That goat grew pale and green with fright.
C
F
He loved that goat, in - deed he did,
The man, he grabbed him by the back
He heaved a sigh as if in pain,
G
C
He loved that goat just like a kid.
And tied him to a rail - road track.
Coughed up those shirts and flagged the train.

JIMMY CRACK CORN

Note/Rote Song

American Folk Song

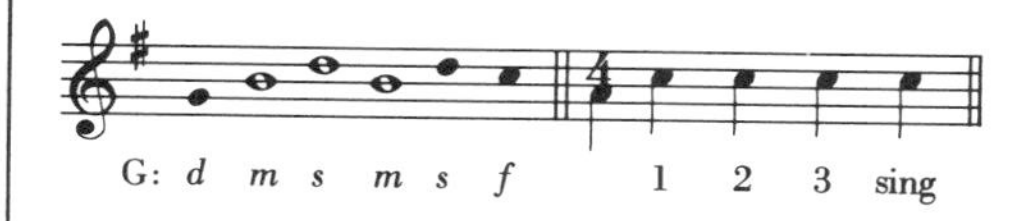

G: d m s m s f
1 2 3 sing

A rest is a sign of silence.
Find — a half-beat rest.
— a one-beat rest.
— a two-beat rest.

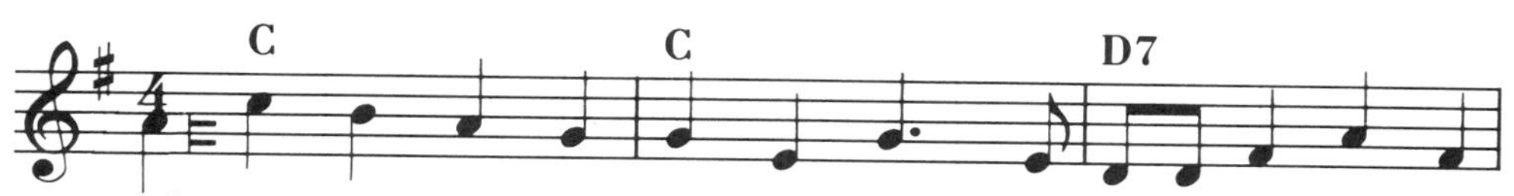

C
C
D7

1. Big old owl with eyes so bright, On man-y a dark and
2. Said the black-bird to the crow: —"Down to the corn-field

G
C
C

star - ry night, I've of - ten heard my true love say,
let us go. Pulling up corn has been our trade,

D7
G
Chorus
G

"Sing all night and sleep all day."
ever since Adam and Eve were made." Jim-my crack corn an'

D7
D7
G

I don't care. Jim-my crack corn an' I don't care.

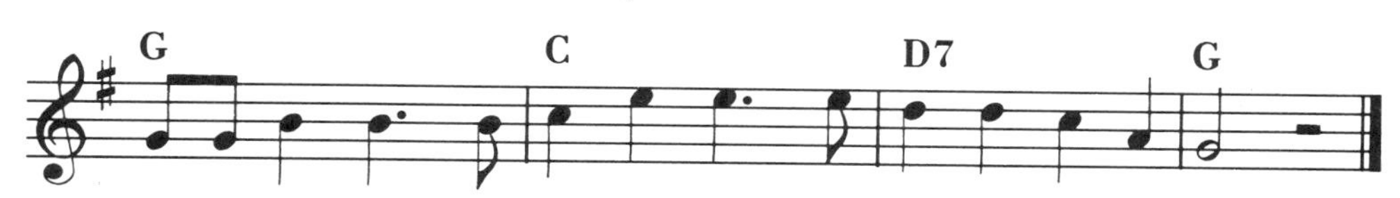

G
C
D7
G

Jim-my crack corn an' I don't care, my mas-ter's gone a-way.

3. Said the sheldrake to the crane:
"When do you think we'll have some rain?
The farm's so muddy and the brook so dry,
If it wasn't for the tadpoles, we'd all die."

4. When I was a boy I used to wait
On master's table and pass the plate.
Hand 'round the bottle when he got dry.
And brush away the blue-tail fly.

LULLABY OF THE IROQUOIS

Rote Song

Music by Vera Russell/Lyrics by Pauline Johnson

Em(G): d t, l, d m d l,
1 2 1 sing

Lit - tle brown ba - by bird lapped in your nest, Wrapped in your nest,
Strapped in your nest, Your straight lit - tle cra - dle board rocks you to
rest. Its hands are your nest, Its bands are your nest, It swings from the
down-bend - ing branch of the oak, You watch the camp-flame and the
curl - ing grey smoke; But oh, for your pret - ty black eyes sleep is
best, Lit - tle brown ba - by of mine, go to rest.

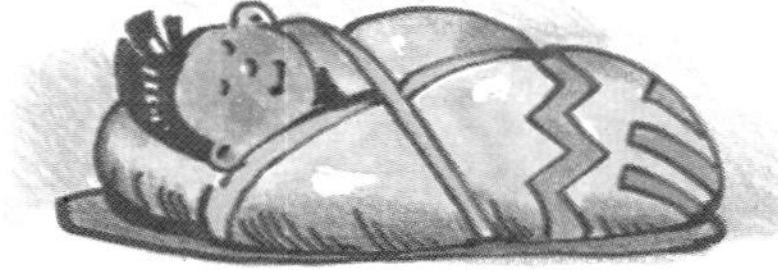

THE THREE BEARS

Rote Song

Arr. by Louise Cullen

C: d' t l s d' l s d'
1 2 3 sing

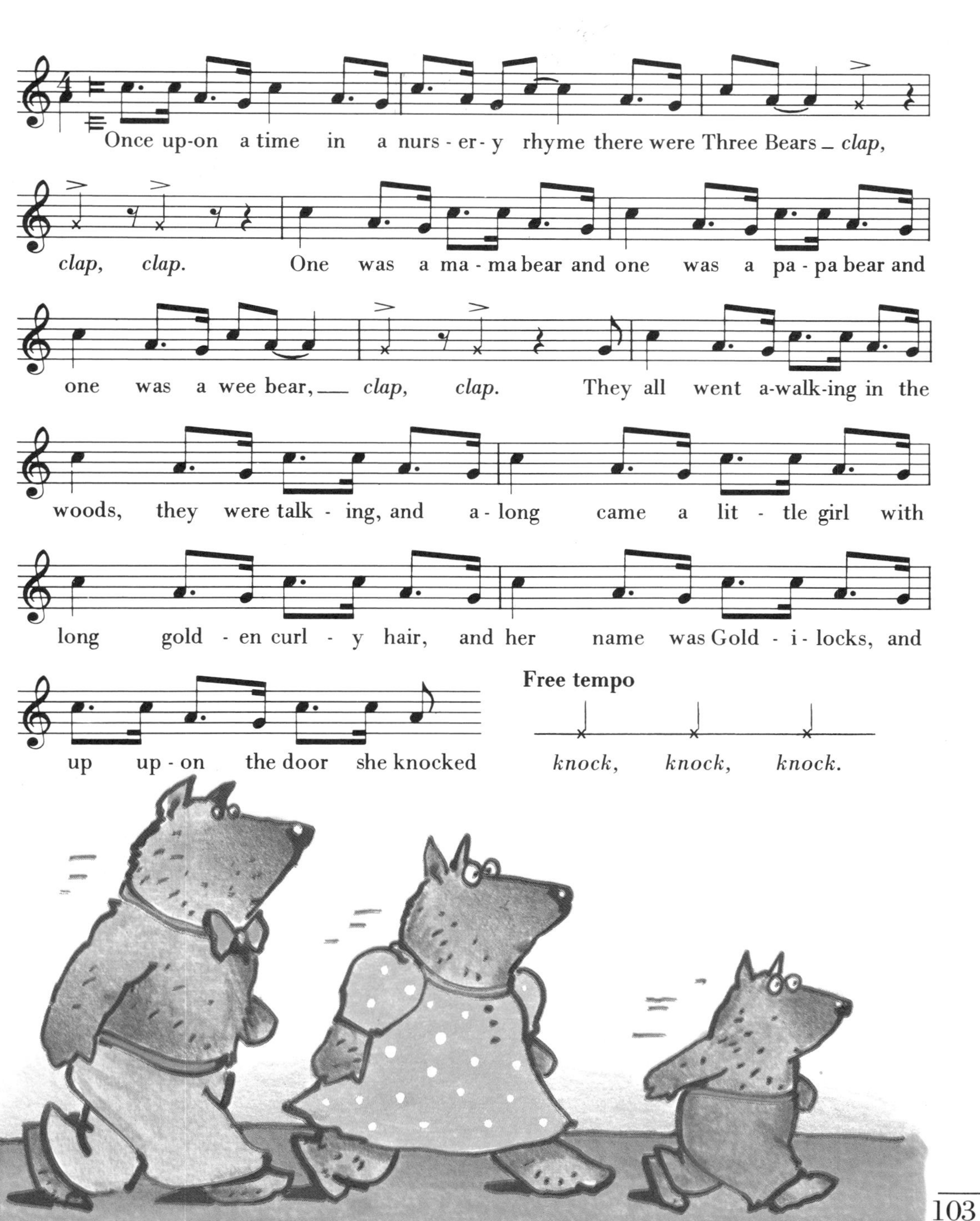
Once up-on a time in a nurs - er - y rhyme there were Three Bears _ clap,
clap, clap. One was a ma - ma bear and one was a pa - pa bear and
one was a wee bear, _ clap, clap. They all went a-walk-ing in the
woods, they were talk - ing, and a - long came a lit - tle girl with
long gold - en curl - y hair, and her name was Gold - i - locks, and
up up - on the door she knocked
Free tempo
knock, knock, knock.

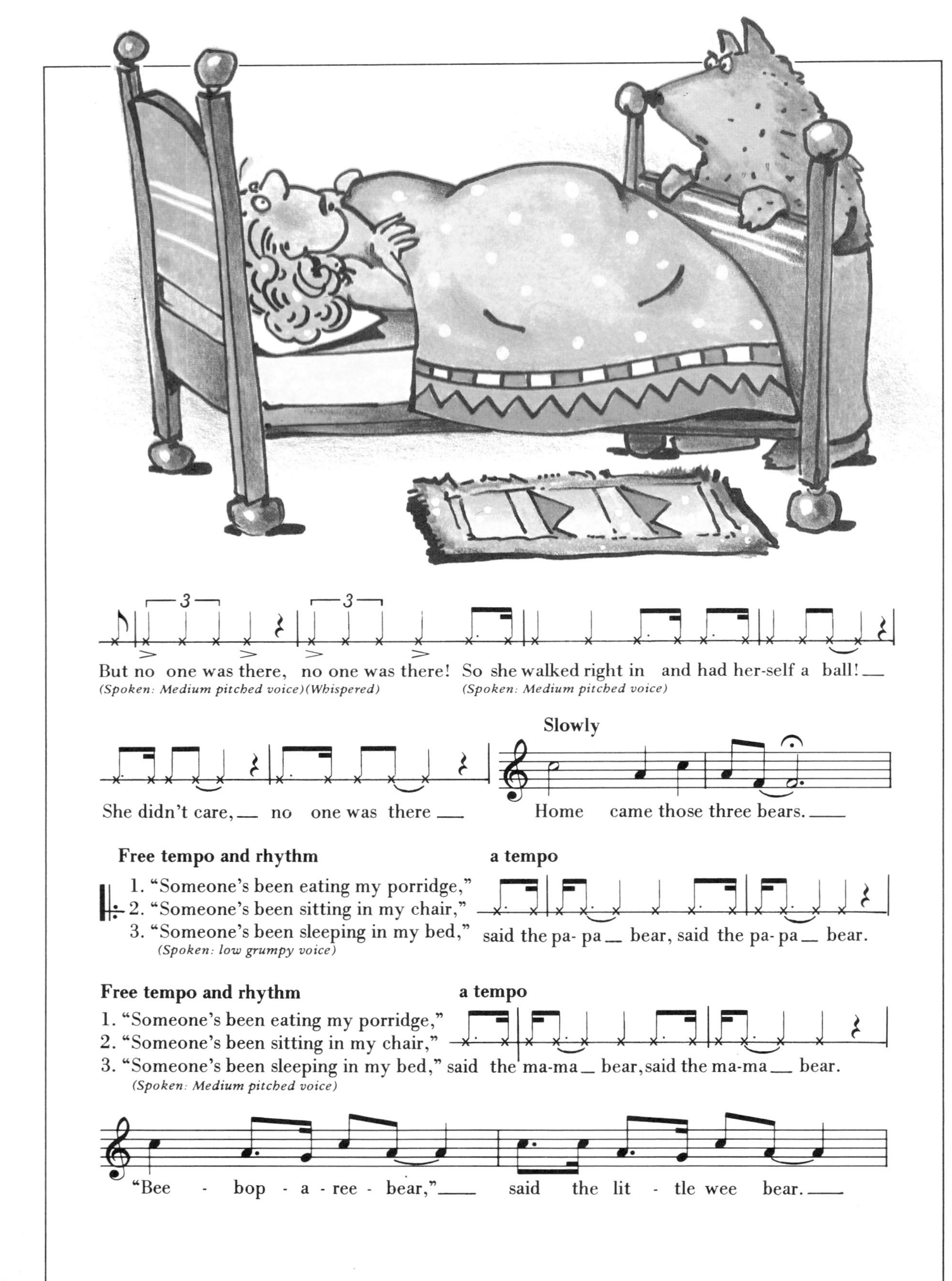
But no one was there, no one was there! So she walked right in and had her-self a ball!
(Spoken: Medium pitched voice) (Whispered)
(Spoken: Medium pitched voice)
She didn't care, no one was there
Slowly
Home came those three bears.
Free tempo and rhythm
a tempo
1. "Someone's been eating my porridge,"
2. "Someone's been sitting in my chair,"
3. "Someone's been sleeping in my bed,"
said the pa-pa bear, said the pa-pa bear.
(Spoken: low grumpy voice)
Free tempo and rhythm
a tempo
1. "Someone's been eating my porridge,"
2. "Someone's been sitting in my chair,"
3. "Someone's been sleeping in my bed," said the ma-ma bear, said the ma-ma bear.
(Spoken: Medium pitched voice)
"Bee - bop - a - ree - bear," said the lit - tle wee bear.

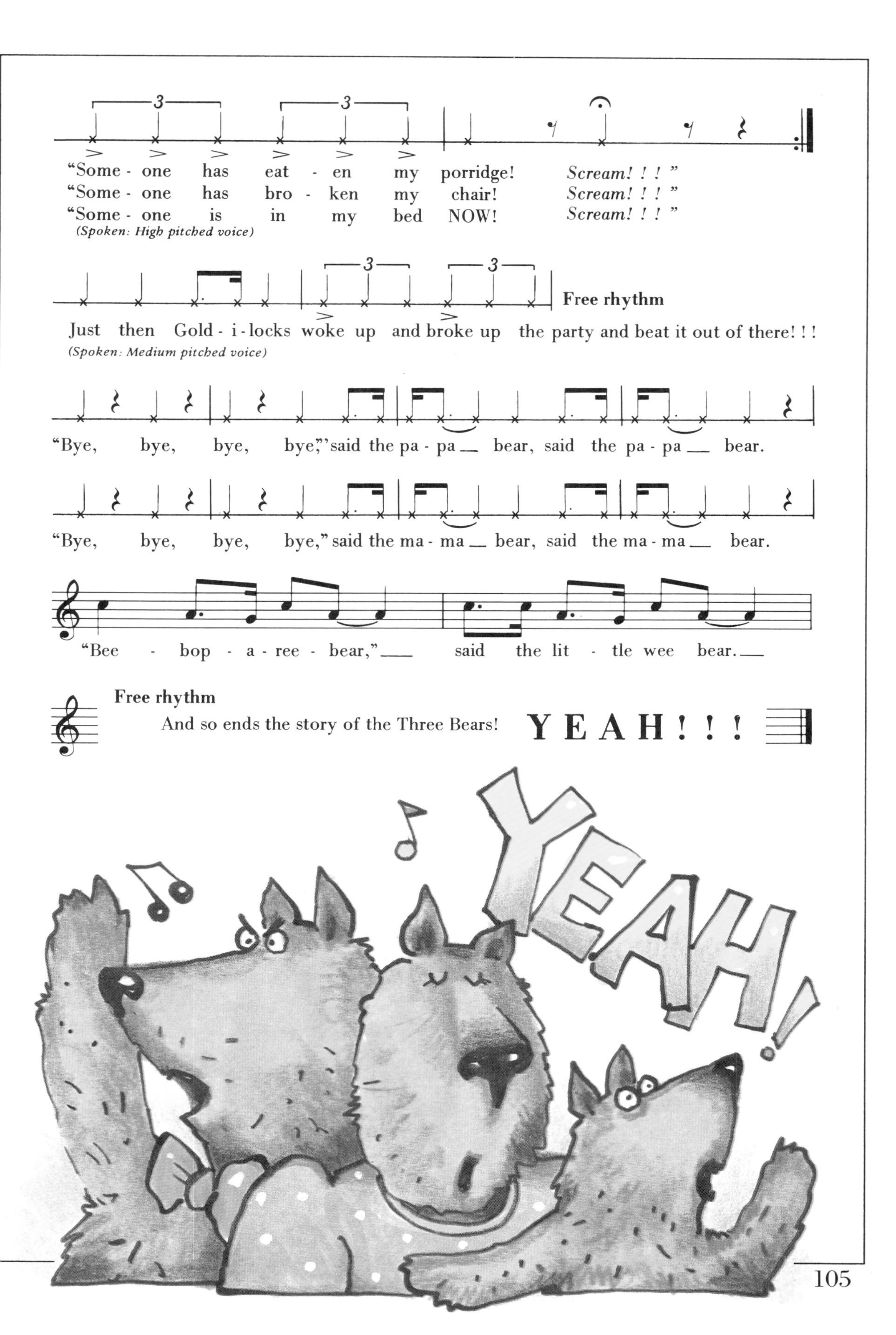
"Some - one has eat - en my porridge! Scream! ! ! "
"Some - one has bro - ken my chair! Scream! ! ! "
"Some - one is in my bed NOW! Scream! ! ! "
(Spoken: High pitched voice)
Just then Gold - i - locks woke up and broke up the party and beat it out of there! ! !
Free rhythm
(Spoken: Medium pitched voice)
"Bye, bye, bye, bye," said the pa - pa __ bear, said the pa - pa __ bear.
"Bye, bye, bye, bye," said the ma - ma __ bear, said the ma - ma __ bear.
"Bee - bop - a - ree - bear," __ said the lit - tle wee bear. __
Free rhythm
And so ends the story of the Three Bears! YEAH ! ! !
YEAH!

RHYTHM SQUARES

Start on any corner square.
Follow the arrows.
Read all the squares aloud using time names without missing a beat.

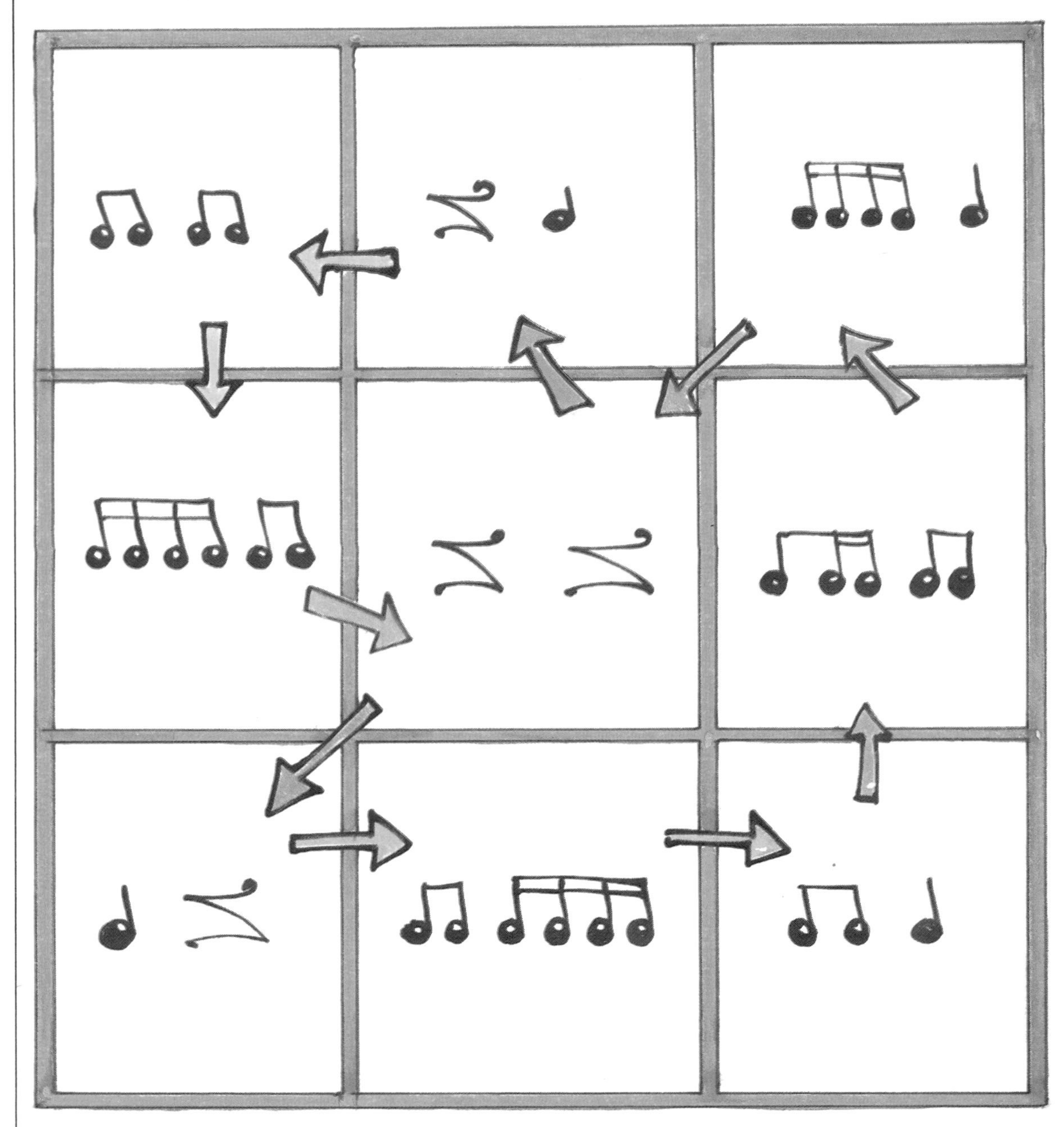

Divide into two groups.
Group 1 uses high speaking voices.
Group 2 uses low speaking voices.

Each group should start on a different corner square.
Follow the arrows.
Read all the squares.

THE HANSTEAD BOYS

Note Song

Canadian Folk Song/Lyrics adapted by B. Andress

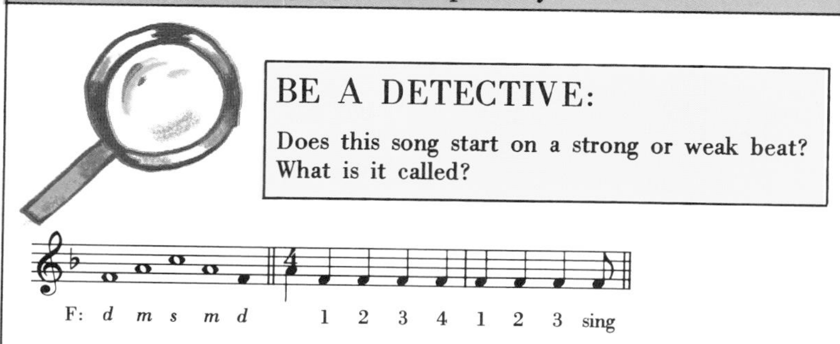

BE A DETECTIVE:
Does this song start on a strong or weak beat?
What is it called?
F: d m s m d
1 2 3 4 1 2 3 sing

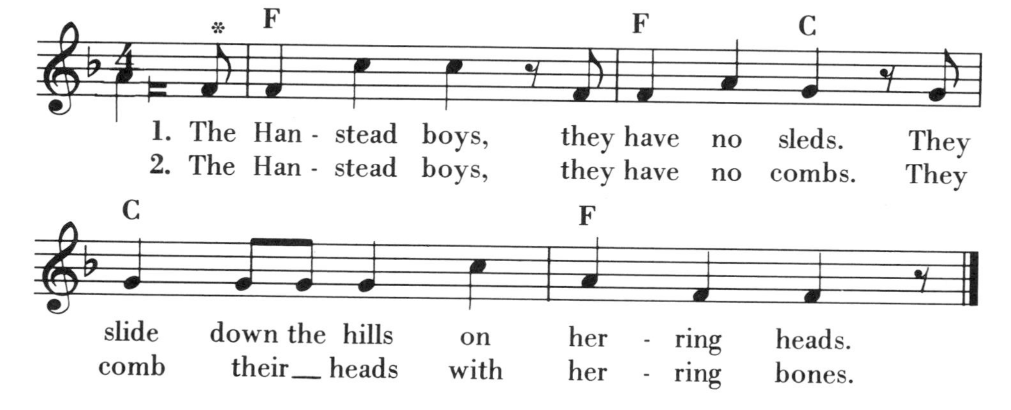

F F C C F
1. The Han - stead boys, they have no sleds. They
2. The Han - stead boys, they have no combs. They
slide down the hills on her - ring heads.
comb their__ heads with her - ring bones.

3. The Hanstead boys, they have no pins.
They mend their coats with old fish fins.

4. The Hanstead boys, they have no nails,
They fix their roofs with old fish scales.

5. The Hanstead boys, they have no pies,
They dine and sup on old fish eyes!

Clap an *ostinato:*

Touch your nose to feel the 𝄾.
Begin on the first strong beat.

fish bones
fish bones

SOMEONE

Rote Song

Music by Charles Winter/Lyrics by Walter de la Mare

Dm(F): d t, l, l, d m d l,
1 2 3 sing

p Dm
A7
Dm
Some-one came knock-ing At my wee, small door;
Dm
Gm
Dm
Some-one came knock-ing, I'm sure, sure, sure;
Dm
Am
Gm
Dm
I list - ened, I op - ened, I looked to left and right,
Dm
A7
Dm
p
But nought there was a - stir-ring in the still dark night;
p Dm
A7
Dm
On - ly the bus - y bee - tle Tap - tap-ping on the wall,
Dm
Gm
Dm
On - ly from the for - est The screech - owl's call,

Dm
Am
Gm
Dm
On - ly the crick-et whist-ling While the dew - drops fall,

Dm
A7
Dm
pp
So I know not who came knock-ing, At all, at all, at all.

This song has markings which will help you make the story interesting.

Use your best singing posture.

p	*piano* – soft
pp	*pianissimo* – very soft
(crescendo sign)	*crescendo* – gradually louder
(diminuendo sign)	*diminuendo* – gradually softer

THE HUM-A-LONG SONG

Rote Song

Dorothy Lees-Blakey

Eb: d' s m d m s
1 2 3 4 1 2 3 sing

1. When-ev-er I hum _ it tick-les my nose, like strings that strum that
2. Hmm ______
hum-ming sound grows. _ From fing-ers and thumb, _ it tick-les and flows, _
and some of the hum ___ goes down to my toes. ______
And sud-den-ly I'm feel-ing hap-py a - gain, just like a
Hmm ______
rain-bow in the rain. So why don't you try ___ my
hum-a-long song? ___ When things go wrong, _ come hum - a - long. _

Stand straight with your hands clasped behind you. Keep your hands clasped and bend over completely so your nose nearly touches your knees. Your knees should be almost straight.
Sing the second verse this way to make a hum that will tickle your nose.

BOYS' DAY

Note Song

Japanese Folk Song/English Lyrics by M. Trotter

E♭: d' s m d m
1 2 3 1 2 sing

1. *Ya ne yo ri ta ka i ko i no bo - ri.*
2. Ev'-ry boy on Boys' Day has pa-per carp to__ fly.

O o ki i ma go i wa o to sa n.
Red and black they show the strength of fear-less Sa- mu - rai.

Chorus

Chi i sa i hi go i wa ko do mo ta__ chi.
Cour-age strong to be a man, oh cour-age we will show.

O mo shi ro so ni o yo i de ru.
Like the bold carp of the sea brave-ly on we go.

3. Higher than the roof-top high paper carp will fly,
Fighting wind as in the sea they fight the waves or die.

4. Father carp so big and black, little carp so red,
Give the message: Be not weak. Be strong instead!

THE LITTLE SKUNK

Rote Song

Canadian Camp Song

B♭: d m d s, 1 2 1 sing

B♭ E♭
1. Oh, I stuck my head in a lit - tle skunk's hole,
2. Oh, I didn't take it out and the lit - tle skunk said,
F B♭
And the lit - tle skunk said, "Well bless my soul!
"If you don't take it out you'll wish you had!
B♭ B♭
Take it out! Take it out!
Take it out! Take it out!
F B♭
Take it out! Re - move it!"
Pheew! I re - moved it!

When you know the song well, clap this rhythm as you sing.
Begin clapping on the word "stuck."

MESTRE ANDRÉ

Rote Song

Portuguese Folk Song/English Lyrics by M. Trotter

G: d m s m d s, 1 2 sing

This is a **cumulative** song. For every verse repeat line 2 of earlier verses until all have been sung again.

Solo
G
D
1. Foi na lo - ja do mes - tr'An - dré que eu com -
2. It was from ___ Mis - ter An - dré I
G
D
prei um tam - bor - zin - ho. Chi-ri - bi - ri - bo um tam - bor -
bought my tam - bou - rine. ___ Ting-a-ling- a - ling my tam - bou-
G
Echo
D
G
zin - ho. Chi-ri - bi - ri - bo um tam - bor - zin - ho.
rine. ___ Ting - a - ling - a - ling my tam - bou - rine. ___
Chorus
D7
G
D7
G
Ai - ó - lé, ai - ó - lé, Foi na lo ja do mes-tr'An-dré.
Ai - ó - lé, ai - ó - lé, At the store of ___ Sir An- dré.
D7
G
D7
G
Ai - ó - lé, ai - ó - lé, Foi na lo - ja do mes-tr' An-dré.
Ai - ó - lé, ai - ó - lé, At the store of ___ Sir An-dré.

3. my violin. Fiddle diddle dee, my violin.
4. my clarinet. Doodle doodle det, my clarinet.
5. my new french horn. So forlorn, my new french horn.
6. my big bass drum. Boom ba-di boom, my big bass drum.

You'll find pictures of these instruments on pages 114 and 115.
Make up new verses by choosing other instruments. To what family do they belong?

FAMILIES OF INSTRUMENTS

Percussion Family

String Family

Woodwind Family
Brass Family

SONG OF THE TRAIN

David McCord

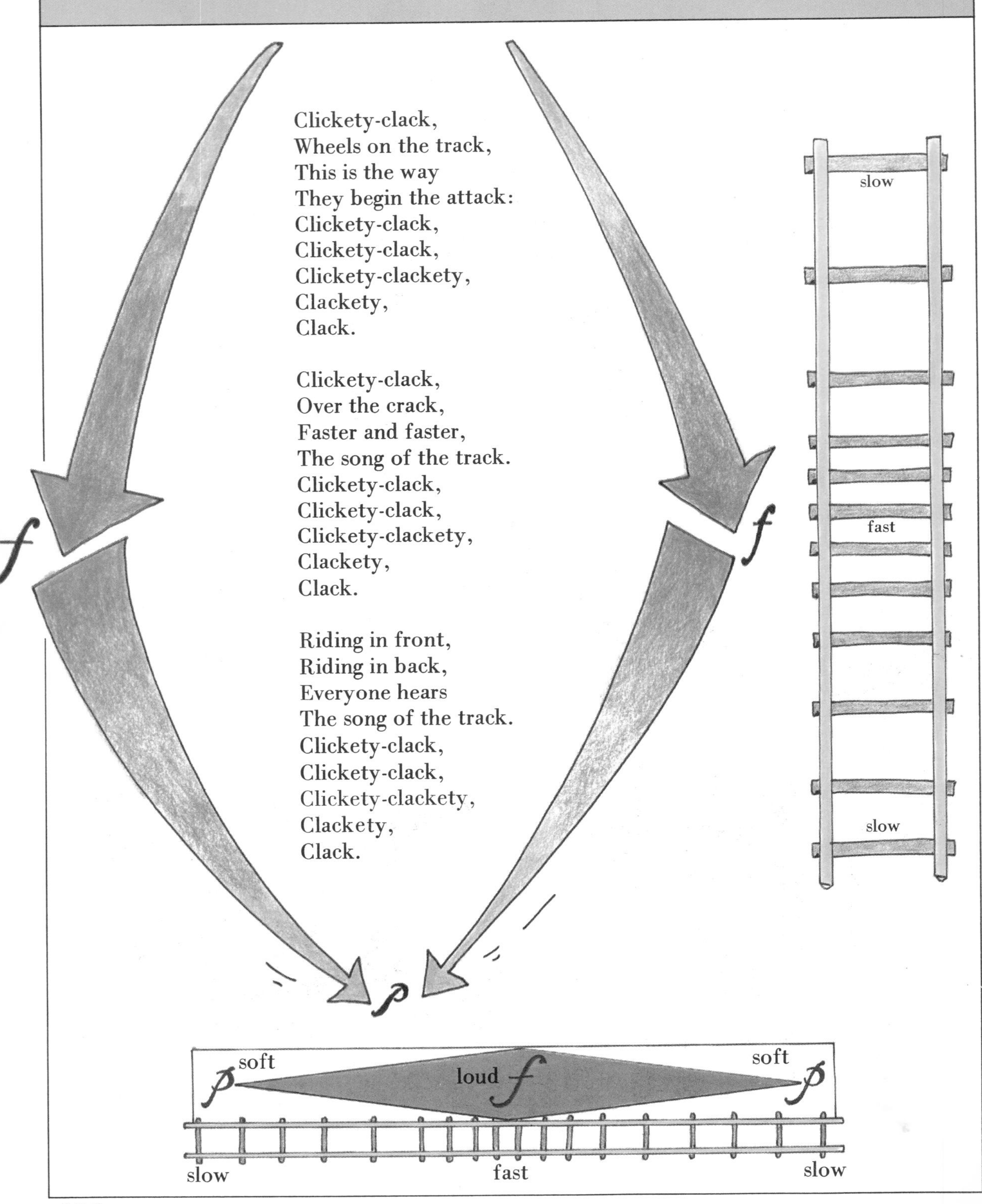
slow
fast
slow
soft
loud
soft
slow
fast
slow

Clickety-clack,
Wheels on the track,
This is the way
They begin the attack:
Clickety-clack,
Clickety-clack,
Clickety-clackety,
Clackety,
Clack.

Clickety-clack,
Over the crack,
Faster and faster,
The song of the track.
Clickety-clack,
Clickety-clack,
Clickety-clackety,
Clackety,
Clack.

Riding in front,
Riding in back,
Everyone hears
The song of the track.
Clickety-clack,
Clickety-clack,
Clickety-clackety,
Clackety,
Clack.

MORNINGTOWN RIDE

Note/Rote Song

Malvina Reynolds

C: d' s m d m
1 2 3 sing

How does the motion of this train make you feel? Compare it with the motion you felt in "Song of the Train."

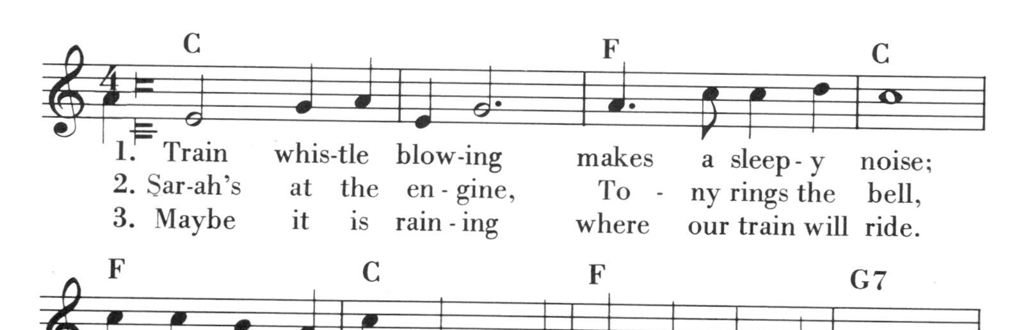
C F C
F C F G7

1. Train whis-tle blow-ing makes a sleep-y noise;
2. Şar-ah's at the en-gine, To-ny rings the bell,
3. Maybe it is rain-ing where our train will ride.

Un-der-neath their blan-kets go all the girls and boys.
John _ swings the lan-tern to show that all is well.
All the lit-tle travel-lers are snug and warm in-side.

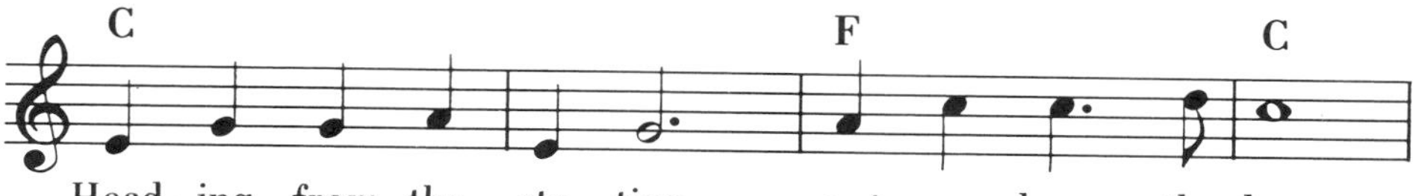
C F C

Head-ing from the sta-tion, out a-long the bay,
Rock-ing, roll-ing, rid-ing out a-long the bay,
Some-where there is sun-shine, some-where there is day.

F C G7 C

All bound for Morn-ing-town, man-y miles a-way.
All bound for Morn-ing-town, man-y miles a-way.
Somewhere there is Morn-ing-town, man-y miles a-way.

BARNYARD SONG

Rote Song

Kentucky Mountain Song

D: d' s m d m s
1 2 1 sing

This music moves in twos and threes.
How do you know when to change?

1. I had a cat and the cat pleased me, I
2. I had a hen and the hen pleased me, I

fed my cat un - der yon - der tree.
fed my hen un - der yon - der tree.

3. duck . . . 5. sheep . . .
4. goose . . . 6. hog . . .

1st Chorus
2nd Chorus
Cat goes Fid-dle-i-fee!
Hen goes Chim-my chuck! Chim-my chuck!

Cat goes Fid-dle-i - fee!
3rd Chorus
Duck goes Quack, Quack!
Hen goes Chim-my chuck! Chim-my chuck! Cat goes Fid-dle-i-fee.
4th Chorus
Goose goes Swish - y, Swash - y! Duck goes Quack, Quack!
Hen goes Chim-my chuck! Chim-my chuck! Cat goes Fid-dle-i-fee!
5th Chorus
Sheep goes Baa, Baa! Goose goes Swish - y, Swash - y!
Duck goes Quack, Quack! Hen goes Chim-my chuck! Chim-my chuck!
Cat goes Fid-dle-i - fee!
6th Chorus
Hog goes Grif- fy, Gruf-fy!
Sheep goes Baa, Baa! Goose goes Swish-y, Swash-y! Duck goes Quack, Quack!
Hen goes Chim-my chuck! Chim-my chuck! Cat goes Fid-dle-i-fee!

MYSTERY SONG

How many different notes are in this song?
What **scale** does it belong to?

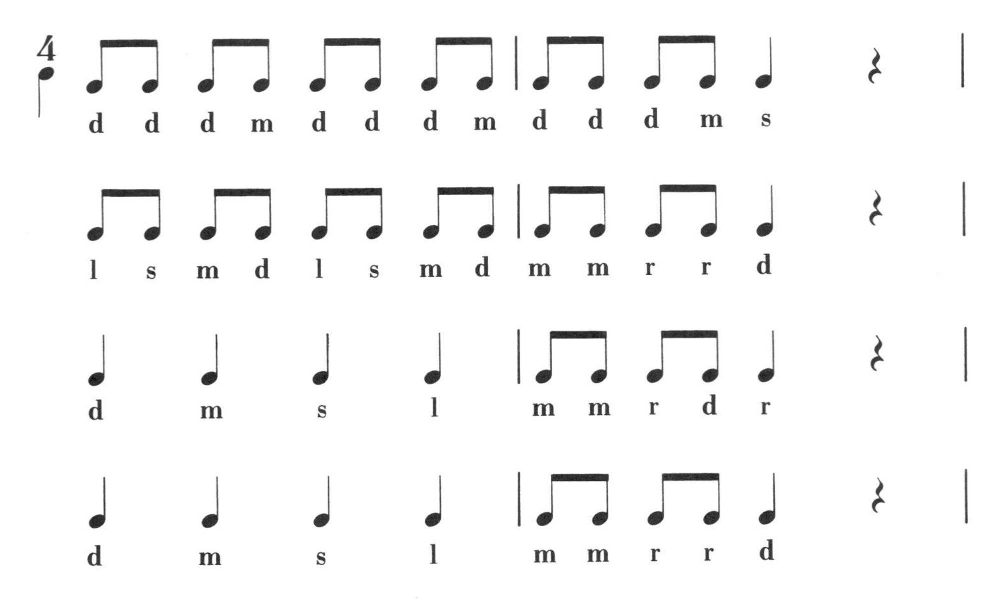
4
d d d m d d d m d d d m s
l s m d l s m d m m r r d
d m s l m m r d r
d m s l m m r r d

Try playing it on the **black keys** of the piano.
Do you know the mystery tune?

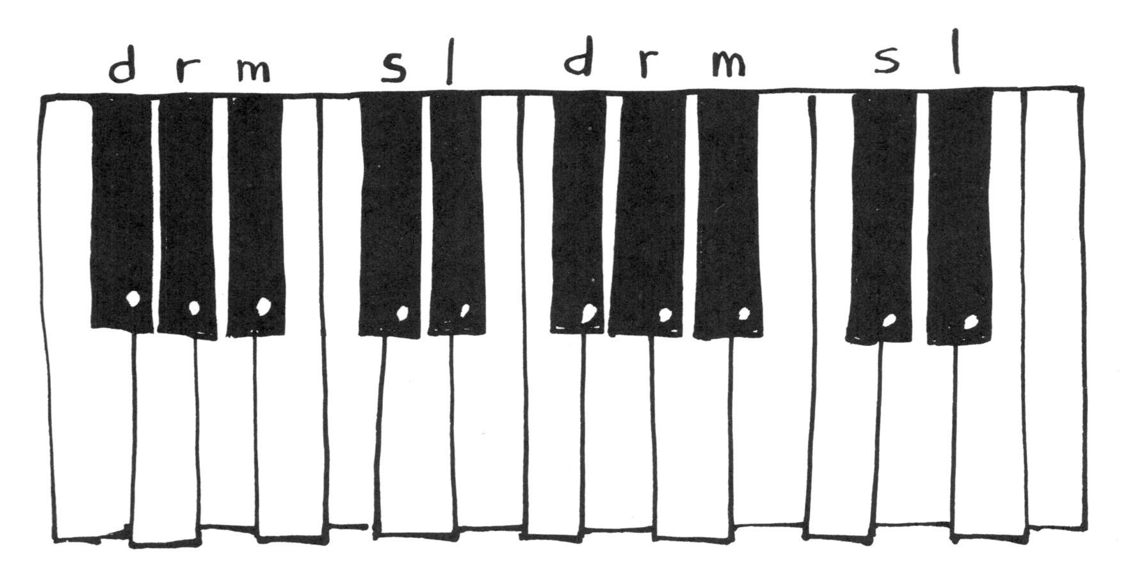
d r m s l d r m s l

THE CRANE

Note Song

Ukrainian Folk Song/English Lyrics by M. Trotter

F: d m s m d s, d
1 2 1 sing

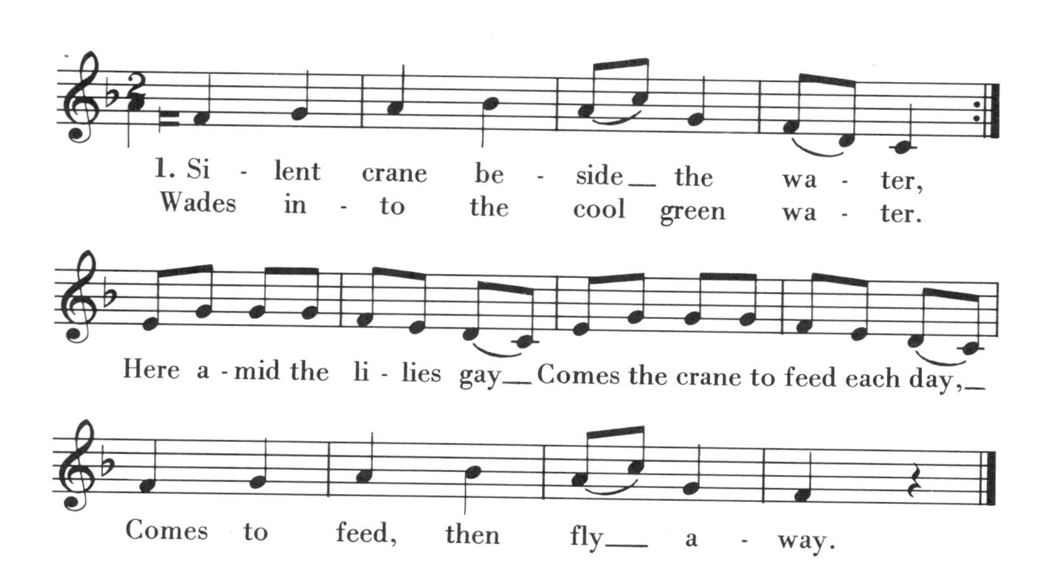

1. Si - lent crane be - side__ the wa - ter,
Wades in - to the cool green wa - ter.
Here a - mid the li - lies gay__ Comes the crane to feed each day,__
Comes to feed, then fly__ a - way.

2. Crane so proud of such great beauty,
Spreads his wings of mighty beauty,
Lord of marshes standing tall,
Sounds his mighty trumpet call
Claiming to be lord of all.

I GOT SHOES

Note Song

Spiritual

G: d m s m d
1 2 3 sing

1. I got shoes, you got shoes, All God's chil-dren got
2. I got wings, you got wings, All God's chil-dren got
shoes. When I get to heav - en, gon - na
wings. When I get to heav - en, gon - na
put on my shoes, An' gon-na walk all ov - er God's
put on my wings, An' gon-na fly all ov - er God's
heav - en, heav - en, heav - en.
heav - en, heav - en, heav - en.
Ev - 'ry bo - dy talk - ing 'bout heav-en ain't go-ing there
Heav - en, heav - en, Gon - na
Heav - en, heav - en, Gon - na

walk all ov - er God's heav - en.
fly all ov - er God's heav - en.

What else might you have when you get to heaven?
Make up your own verses. Add an **ostinato**.

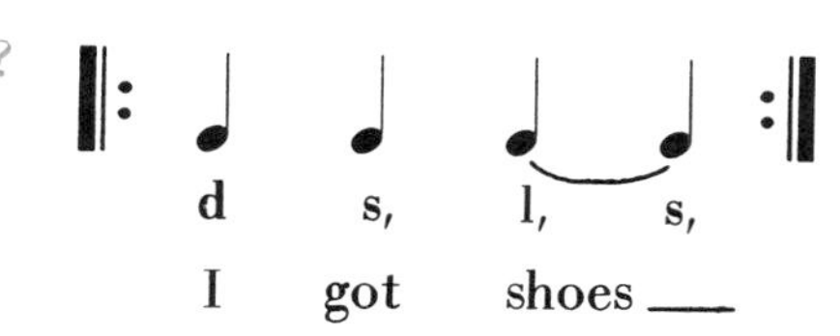
d s, l, s,
I got shoes

PENTATONIC PUZZLE

Pentatonic scales have five different notes and one octave note.
The **doh pentatonic scale** goes from **doh** to **doh′**.

d r m s l d′

Sing the **doh pentatonic scale** using hand signs.
Sing the scale descending from **doh′** to **doh**.

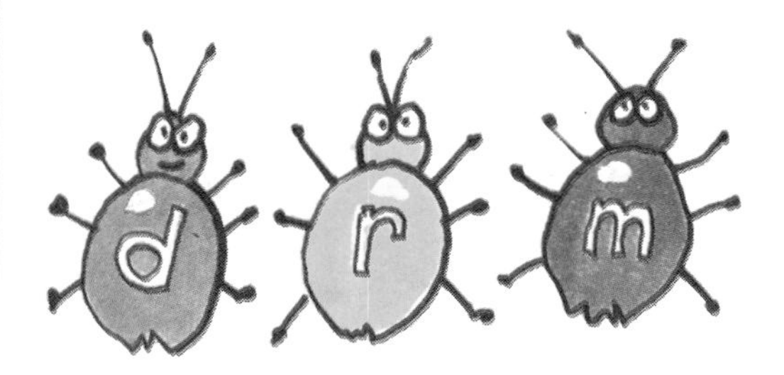
d
r
m

s
l

d′

What would you call a **pentatonic scale** that goes from **lah,** to **lah**?

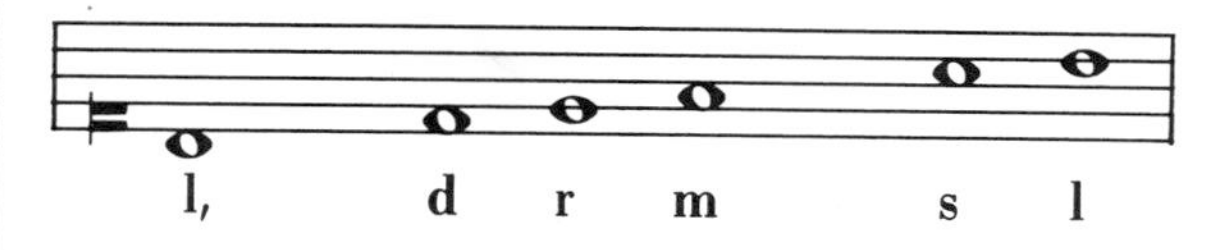
l, d r m s l

Sing this **pentatonic scale** using handsigns.
Sing the scale descending from **lah** to **lah,**.

OJIBWA SONG

Note/Rote Song

Native Peoples' Song

What note starts this song?
What note ends it?
What other notes are used?
What **scale** is used?

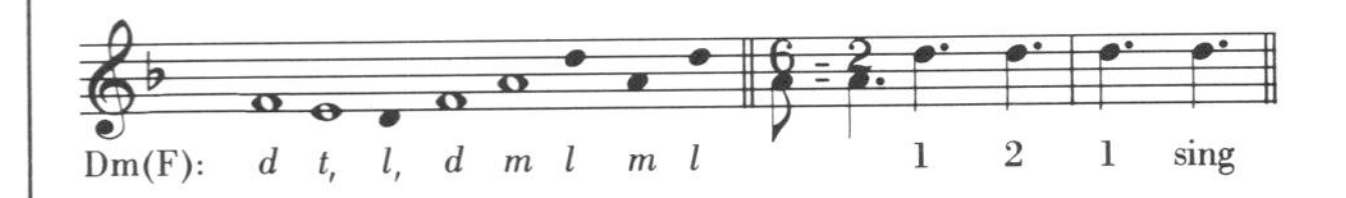

Dm(F): d t, l, d m l m l
1 2 1 sing

Ki-a-na me-a ko-nu, Ki-a-na me-a ko-nu,
Ki-o-ke-na Ha Tu-no, Ki-o-ke-na Ha Tu-no.

Map the **phrases** in the air as you sing.

How are the phrases similar? different?
What happens to the **melody**?

AYII, AYII, AYII

Poem Song

Inuit

Ayii, ayii, ayii,
My arms, they wave high in the air,
My hands, they flutter behind my back,
They wave above my head
Like the wings of a bird.
Let me move my feet.
Let me dance.
Let me shrug my shoulders.
Let me shake my body.
Let me crouch down.
My arms, let me fold them.
Let me hold my hands under my chin.

LISTENING:

"Signs of the Zodiac" from *The Adventures of Mercury*

Eric Satie

This piece is like a game that plays with three musical ideas.
The ideas look like this:

ZODIAC
1
2
3

The trumpet, tuba and violins take turns playing these ideas.

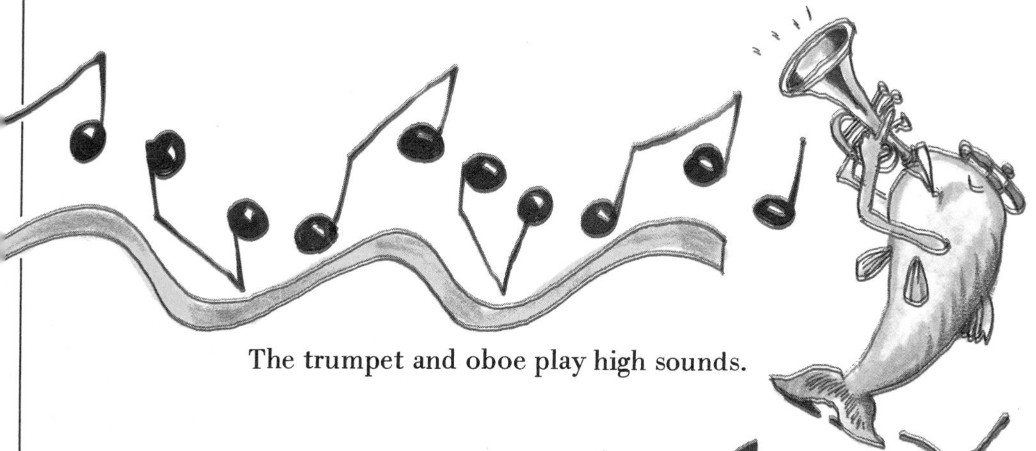

The trumpet and oboe play high sounds.

The violins play high sounds.

The tuba plays low sounds.

Pretend you play one of these instruments.

When you hear your instrument play, map the musical idea you hear in the air.

PURPLE STEW

Note/Rote Song

Canadian Game Song

F: d r m r d r
1 2 3 sing

Mak-ing a pur - ple stew (whip, whip, whip, whip).
Mak-ing a pur - ple stew, (scoo-by doo-by) with
Pur-ple po-ta-toes and pur-ple to-ma-toes and
e - ven a pur - ple you!
Fan-cy meet-in' you in a pur-ple stew!

Play the game:

Form a circle with one person in the centre.
Everyone sings the song and pretends to stir a huge pot of stew.
With one hand, throw in the potatoes; with the other, the tomatoes.
On the words "even a purple you," the person in the centre spins around with closed eyes and one arm pointing out. The centre person stops on the word "you." The person to whom he/she's pointing takes the place in the centre.

HANSEL AND GRETEL: AN OPERA

An **opera** is a way of telling a story through music. Singers and dancers tell the story from the stage, and an orchestra plays in the pit to accompany them and to create musical **moods**.

BROTHER, COME AND DANCE

Rote Song

E. Humperdinck

These two songs are from the opera *Hansel and Gretel.*

While alone at home, Hansel and Gretel were tired of working and started to dance and sing. Their mother returned and scolded them for playing while she was out. During their argument, a pitcher of milk was broken – the only food in the house. In her anger, their mother sent them to find berries for dinner.

F: d m s m d m s 1 2 1 sing
F C
Broth - er, come and dance with me, Both my hands I
F B♭ C
give to thee, Right foot first, left foot then, 'Round a-bout and
F F
back a - gain. With your feet you tap, tap, tap,
With your head you nick, nick, nick,
B♭ C7
With your hands you clap, clap, clap, Right foot first,
With your fin - gers click, click, click, Right foot first,
F C7 C6 F
left foot then, 'Round a - bout and back a - gain.
left foot then, 'Round a - bout and back a - gain.

THERE STANDS A LITTLE MAN

Rote Song

E. Humperdinck

Hansel and Gretel wandered deep into the woods looking for berries. As night began to fall, they realized they were lost. It was then they met a little man. Who do you think he was?

F: d m s m d s,
1 2 1 sing

F
C
1. There stands a lit - tle man in the wood a -
2. His hair is all of gold and his cheeks are
F
F
lone, He wears a lit - tle man - tle of
red, He wears a lit - tle black cap up -
C
F
F
vel - vet brown. Say, who can the
on his head. Say, who can the
C
F
C
man - kin be, Stand - ing there be - neath the tree
man - kin be, Stand - ing there so si - lent - ly,
F
F
C
F
With the lit - tle man - tle of vel - vet brown?
With the lit - tle black_cap up - on his head?

Hansel and Gretel had quite an adventure after their evening in the forest. What do you think happened to them?

A FLOCK OF LITTLE BOATS

Samuel Menashe

END
START

A flock of little boats
Tethered to the shore
Drifts in still water
Prows dip, nibbling.

A poet paints a picture
with words.
A musician paints
with sounds.

Paint a sailboat picture in sound using these ideas:

- whisper "Chuckle-chuckle" (waves lapping against the hull)
- rub palms together (water running over deck)
- snap fingers (wind snapping sheets)
- whisper (wind) <whoo>
- <sh sh sh> (swells rushing)

THREE SAILORS

Rote Song

Katherine Davis

C: d' s m d m s
1 2 1 sing

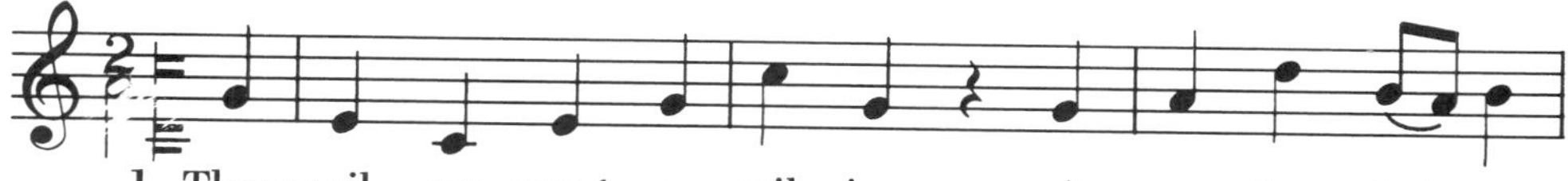

1. Three sail - ors went a - sail - ing A - cross the brin- y
2. And first they caught a min - now And put it in __ a

sea, A - cross the brin- y sea, And one was nine, and __
pail, And put it in __ a pail, And then they caught a ___

one was five, And _ one was on - ly three. Yo ho! Yo
lob - ster, ___ And then they caught a whale! Yo ho! Yo

ho! Yo ho, yo, ho, yo ho! And _ one was on - ly three!
ho! Yo ho, yo, ho, yo ho! And then they caught a whale!

3. And then they had a shipwreck
Upon a desert isle,
Upon a desert isle,
And lived on bark and berries
For quite a little while.
Yo ho! Yo ho! Yo ho, yo ho, yo ho!
For quite a little while!

4. But just when they were starving
And growing thin and thinner,
And growing thin and thinner,
Their mother came to the kitchen door
And called them in to dinner,
Yo ho! Yo ho! Yo ho, yo ho, yo ho!
And called them in to dinner.

5. The sailors swam to meet her,
Across the grassy sea,
Across the grassy sea,
And one was nine, and one was five,
And one was only three.
Yo ho! Yo ho! Yo ho, yo ho, yo ho!
And one was only three.

GRANDPA'S WHISKERS

Rote Song

Composer Unknown

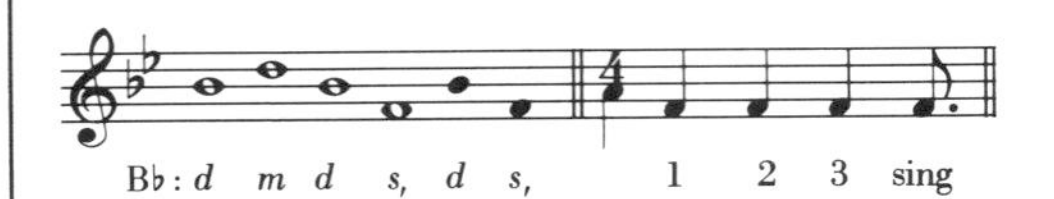
B♭: d m d s, d s,
1 2 3 sing

B♭
Cm/E♭
1. I have a dear old grand-pa, His hair is turn-ing gray,
2. I have a dear old un - cle, He drives a Ford ma-chine,

F7
F
B♭
He has a pair of whisk-ers, They're al - ways in the way. Oh!
He u - ses grand-pa's whisk-ers to strain the gas - o - line. Oh!

Chorus

B♭
Cm/E♭
They're al - ways in the way. The cows eat them for hay.

F7
F7
B♭
They cov-er the dirt on grand-pa's shirt, They're al - ways in the way.

3. I have a dear old grandma,
And every night she sleeps,
She chews on grandpa's whiskers,
And dreams it's shredded wheat. Oh!

4. Ev'ry Sunday morning
We gather in a group,
To watch old grandpa's whiskers
A-dangling in the soup. Oh!

O CANADA

Rote Song

Music by A.C. Lavalée/English Lyrics by R.S. Weir/French Lyrics by A. Routhier

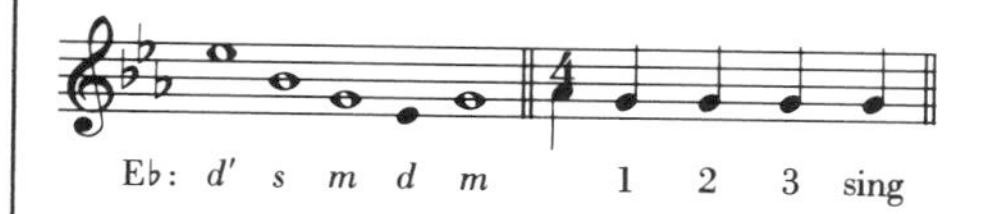

Eb: d' s m d m
1 2 3 sing

O Can - a - da! Our home and na - tive land,
True pa - triot love in all thy sons com mand.
With glow - ing hearts we see thee rise, The
true North, strong and free; From far and wide, O
Can - a - da, we stand on guard for thee.
God keep our land Glo - rious and free!
O Can - a - da! we stand on guard for thee,
O Can - a - da! we stand on guard for thee.

O Canada! Terre de nos aieux,
Ton front est ceint de fleurons glorieux!
Car ton bras sait porter l'épée
Il sait porter la croix!

Ton histoire est une épopée des plus brillants exploits.
Et ta valeur, de foi trempée.
Protégera nos foyers et nos droits,
Protégera nos foyers et nos droits.

ACKNOWLEDGEMENTS

Care has been exercised to trace ownership of copyright material contained in this text. The publishers will gladly receive information that will enable them to rectify any reference or credit in subsequent editions.
Pg. 2 ZIP-A-DEE-DOO-DAH Words & Music by: Ray Gilbert Music by: Allie Wrubel © 1945 Walt Disney Music Company. Pg. 7 ALOUETTE by Edith Fowke Reprinted from *Folk Songs of Canada*, Waterloo Music Company. Pg. 8 THE BIRTHDAY CHILD Reprinted by permission of Holt, Rinehart and Winston, Publishers, New York, N.Y. Pg. 10 JOHNNY ONE HAMMER Reprinted by permission of Holt, Rinehart and Winston, Publishers, New York, N.Y. Pg. 11 SAUTE LE PANTIN from Heribert and Johannes Grüger, Die Liederfibel, Duesseldorf 1969, Verlag Schwann. Pg. 14 COY MALINDO From EARLY AMERICAN SONGS adapted by Margaret and Travis Johnson. (Original title I SPURRED MY HORSE) Copyright © 1943 by Associated Music Publishers, Inc., New York, Reprinted by permission of the publisher. Pg. 16 HOT CROSS BUNS © Copyright 1974 by Boosey & Hawkes Inc. Reproduced by permission of Boosey & Hawkes (Canada) Limited. Pg. 18 ALISON'S CAMEL From ELEPHANT JAM. Copyright © Pachyderm Music, 1980. Reprinted by permission of McGraw-Hill Ryerson Limited. Pg. 21 ROCKY MOUNTAIN © Copyright 1974 by Boosey & Hawkes, Inc. Reproduced by permission of Boosey & Hawkes (Canada) Limited. Pg. 22 COLOUR A RAINBOW by Dorothy Cameron Smith taken from The Seasons of Children. Pg. 23 AN IROQUOIS LULLABY from *Canada's Story in Song* by Edith Fowke and Alan Mills, © Gage Publishing 1965. Reprinted by permission. Pg. 23 AN IROQUOIS LULLABY French text from LES CHANSONS DE "CHEZ HELENE" by Helene Baillargeon, by permission of Gordon V. Thompson Limited, Toronto. Pg. 24 BEDTIME STORIES by Lilian Moore from Lilian Moore, *See My Lovely Poison Ivy* Copyright © 1975 by Lilian Moore (New York: Atheneum, 1975) Reprinted with the permission of Atheneum Publishers. Pg. 25 SKIN AND BONES by Jean Ritchie 1952 Geordie Music Publishing Co. Pg. 29 WINNIE THE WITCH by Barbara Andress Reprinted by permission of Holt, Rinehart and Winston, Publishers, New York, N.Y. Pg. 31 LITTLE TOMMY TINKER From ELEPHANT JAM. Copyright © Pachyderm Music, 1980. Reprinted by permission of McGraw-Hill Ryerson Limited. Pg. 35 DONKEY RIDING Collected by Thomas Wood (altered by permission). By permission of Oxford University Press. Pg. 36 DOBBIN, DOBBIN by Beatrice and Max Krone From DISCOVERING MUSIC TOGETHER, Volume 4 by Leohard, Krone, Wolfe and Fullerton. Copyright © 1967. Used by permission of Follett Publishing Company. Pg. 38 DO-RE-MI Words by: Oscar Hammerstein 2nd, Music by: Richard Rodgers Copyright © 1959 & 1960 by Richard Rodgers and Oscar Hammerstein 2nd. Williamson Music Inc., New York, N.Y., owner of publication and allied rights for all countries of the Western Hemisphere International copyright secured. ALL RIGHTS RESERVED. Pg. 40 THE MARVELOUS TOY by Tom Paxton © Copyright 1961, 1964 Cherry Lane Music Co. Used by Permission. All Rights Reserved. Pg. 42 BIFFY Reprinted by permission of Holt, Rinehart and Winston, Publishers, New York, N.Y. Pg. 47 JOY TO THE WORLD Neilson et al., *Growing With Music, Book 6* (Englewood Cliffs, N.J. Prentice-Hall) © 1966. Pg. 48 NUTTIN' FOR CHRISTMAS Words and Music by Sid Tepper and Roy C. Bennett. Copyright © 1955 by ANNE-RACHEL MUSIC CORPORATION. Copyright and all rights assigned to CHAPPELL & CO. INC., New York, N.Y. INTERSONG MUSIC publisher. Reprinted by permission of Chappell Music Canada Limited. ALL RIGHTS RESERVED. Pg. 52 THE PIÑATA From MAKING MUSIC YOUR OWN 3, © 1971 General Learning Corporation. Reprinted by permission of Silver Burdett Company. Pg. 55 SONG OF THE CRIB Original title "Joseph, O Dear Joseph Mine" from NOËLS—Marx & Anne Oberndorfer. © H.T. FitzSimons Co. Pg. 56 IT'S CHRISTMAS Words and Music by Dorothy Lees-Blakey. Pg. 57 I'M SUPER, I'M SMART Music: Lancelot Fowler Words: Elizabeth Stenson. Pg. 59 BASSEZ DOWN From ELEPHANT JAM. Copyright © Pachyderm Music, 1980. Reprinted by permission of McGraw-Hill Ryerson Limited. Pg. 67 TOUT CELA EST À MOI Tiré du recueil "PERLIMPINPIN". Edition Foetisch, Lausanne (Suisse). Tous droits réservés. Copie ou reproduction interdites. Pg. 75 MAGIC PENNY Words and Music by MALVINA REYNOLDS © Copyright 1955, 1958 by Northern Music Co. Used by permission. Pg. 82 SCOTLANDS BURNING Lois Choksy, THE KODALY METHOD: Comprehensive Music Education from Infant to Adult, © 1974, p. 176. Adapted by permission of Prentice-Hall, Inc., Englewood Cliffs, N.J. Pg. 85 THE MUDDY PUDDLE From GARBAGE DELIGHT by Dennis Lee. Set to music by permission of Macmillan of Canada. A Division of Gage Publishing Limited. Pg. 86 NEATH THE LILACS From OKKI-TOKKI-UNGA, Action Songs for Children, published by A & C Black Ltd., London. Pg. 89 MAPLE SYRUP Reprinted by permission of the copyright owner, Leslie Music Supply, Oakville, Ontario, Canada. Pg. 93 I'M SO TIRED ALEX LAURIER (CAPAC). Reprinted by permission of Alex Laurier. Pg. 96 MUSIC ALONE SHALL LIVE From "Fifty Canons and Rounds" © 1965, Hargail Music Press. Pg. 98 SARASPONDA Copyright © 1981, Holt, Rinehart and Winston, Publishers, New York, N.Y. Reprinted by permission. Pg. 99 BOOM-DEE-AH-DAH Reprinted by permission of Holt, Rinehart and Winston, Publishers, New York, N.Y. Pg. 100 THE GOAT Reprinted by permission of Holt, Rinehart and Winston, Publishers, New York, N.Y. Pg. 102 LULLABY OF THE IROQUOIS For the poem of the name from FLINT & FEATHER, The Complete Poems of E. Pauline Johnson, Copyrighted and publihsed by Hodder and Stoughton Limited, Toronto, Ontario. Pg. 103 THE THREE BEARS by Louise Cullen Dane. Pg. 107 THE HANSTEAD BOYS Reprinted by permission of Holt, Rinehart and Winston, Publishers, New York, N.Y. Pg. 108 SOMEONE by Walter de la Mare The Literary Trustees of Walter de la Mare and The Society of Authors as their representative. Pg. 110 THE HUM-A-LONG SONG Words and music by Dorothy Lees-Blakey. Reprinted by permission of Dorothy Lees-Blakey. Pg. 112 THE LITTLE SKUNK from SALLY GO ROUND THE SUN by Edith Fowke. Reprinted by permission of The Canadian Publishers, McClelland and Stewart Limited, Toronto. Pg. 117 MORNINGTOWN RIDE Words and Music by Malvina Reynolds © 1957 Amadeo Music. Used by permission of Amadeo Music. Pg. 122 I GOT SHOES From THRESHOLD TO MUSIC (First Edition) Teacher's Text/Manual for Years 1-4 by Mary Helen Richards. Copyright © 1967 by Fearon Publishers, Inc. Reprinted by permission of Pitman Learning Inc., Belmont, California. Pg. 125 AYII, AYII, AYII From SONGS OF THE DREAM PEOPLE by James Houston Pg. 132 A FLOCK OF LITTLE BOATS From TO OPEN by Samuel Menashe Copyright © 1974 by Samuel Menashe. Reprinted by permission of Viking Penguin Inc.

CLASSIFIED INDEX

GAME SONGS

ROUNDS

SPECIAL OCCASION SONGS

Christmas

Hallowe'en

St. Patrick's Day

Thanksgiving

Valentine's Day

ALPHABETICAL INDEX